# Context

Cities are often places of great energy and optimism. They are where most of us choose to live work and interact with others. As a result, **cities are where innovation happens, where ideas are formed from which economic growth largely stems**. Although wrestling with difficult challenges, sometimes individually but more often collectively, cities are able to address some of the most significant challenges facing society today. City councils around the world are reducing air pollution, banning diesel cars, introducing smoking bans, bicycle rental schemes and even imposing sugar taxes in order to help citizens make better lifestyle choices. Often nimbler than nation states, cities such as Paris, London, Mexico City, Aspen and Copenhagen are becoming test-beds for innovation that is then shared from one to another. There is much to be done and many city leaders are working on the challenges.

However, as a steadily rising global population approaches 70% urbanization, the problems are now accelerating. City leaders today have to react quickly to accommodate vast influxes of people. There are many priorities; the provision of basic services - housing, water, sanitation, schools and hospitals; the establishment and maintenance of effective transport and technology infrastructures; the delivery of fair and effective policing; and the creation of an attractive business environment. The list is considerable. Now, perhaps more than ever, city leaders are seeking to better understand, share and explore options and future directions. No two cities are the same, so there is no universal blueprint on how best to design, manage and support urban growth. But experiences can be shared, lessons learned, models debated and new perspectives discussed.

The Future Agenda team facilitated twelve high-level discussions in different cities around the world to explore this topic. This document provides an analysis of these and associated discussions and aims to provide context, highlight issues and provide insights around some of the key opportunities for positive change.

# The Future Agenda

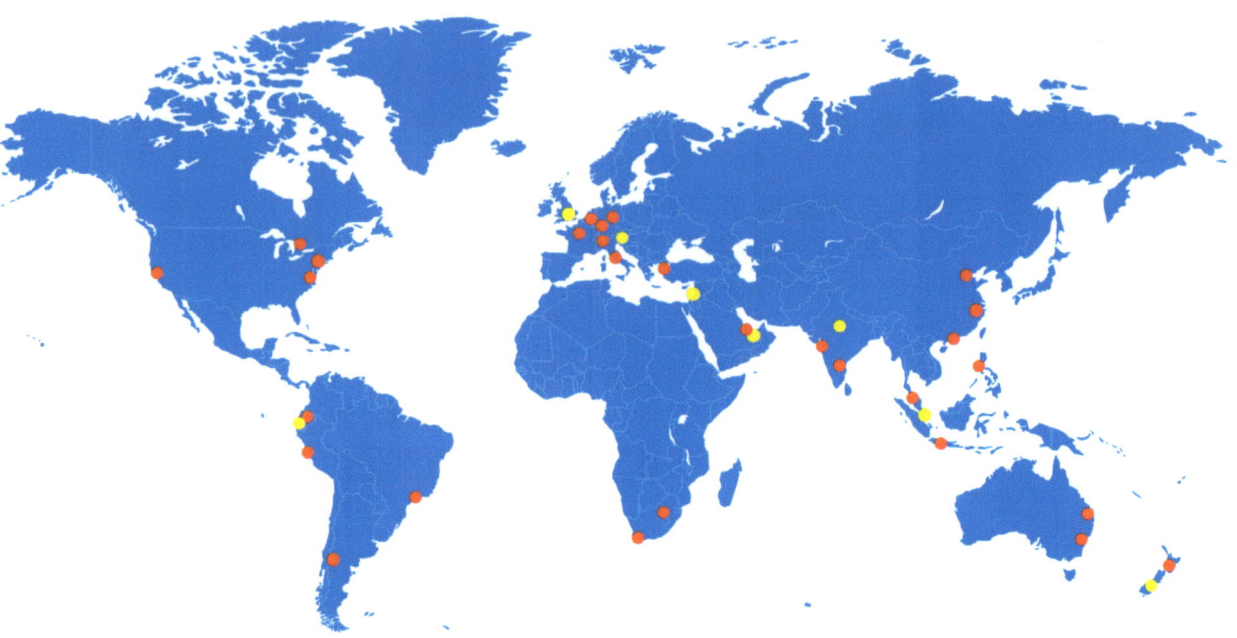

The Future Agenda programme explores the key issues facing society globally over the next 10 years. Its aim is to use workshops and discussion forums to identify ways in which systems will function, consumers will behave and governments will regulate over the next decade. It was created by Growth Agenda to give all organisations, large or small, the opportunity to access insights that will help them decide on future strategy.

In addition to discussions on the Future of Cities, during 2015/16 120 other workshops were held in 45 locations to explore more than 20 critical issues facing society. These included the future of data, the future of health and healthcare, the future of transport and of work. These workshops helped to support, enrich and challenge initial perspectives given by leading experts to the Future Agenda programme. In turn the insights from these sessions were published and shared widely. As a result, we have received further feedback from those outside the workshop process that has provided even greater depth for the analysis which can be found in our final 'Future Agenda: The World in 2025' reports.[1]

In order to gain as diverse a view as possible about the future of cities, workshops were not only held in established urban centres such Singapore, Dubai, Delhi, Mumbai, London and Toronto but we also visited less high-profile locations including Beirut, now a destination for many of the 2m refugees from neighbouring countries; Christchurch, still recovering from a devastating earthquake in 2011; and Guayaquil, the fast-growing Pacific port-city in Ecuador. The resulting discussions between informed individuals from across academia, business, government and NGOs brought together leading views on how urban development may need to change and adapt for the future.

# Summary Insights

Although some points were specific to individual locations, a number of issues were shared across all the discussions. We also heard different views on how the future development of the urban environment should take place.

| Common Challenges | Managing Migration | Countering Inequality | Sustainable Scaling |
|---|---|---|---|
| **Shared Ambitions** | Healthy Cities | Accessible Cities | Intelligent Cities |
| **Emerging Concerns** | Safe Cities | Resilient Cities | Collaborative Co-opetition |

**There are three common challenges:**

*Managing Migration:*
- The facilitation of internal and international migration to cities is set to be one of the defining shifts of the 21st century.

*Countering Inequality:*
- Providing equitable access to all elements of urban life including transport, sanitation, healthcare, education and work to facilitate economic growth and cement social stability.

*Sustainable Scaling:*
- Ensuring the sustainable development of infrastructure, the reduction of pollution and the creation of a safe, healthy environment in a time of accelerated urban expansion.

**Equally, in many cities there are a number of shared future ambitions:**

*Healthy Cities:*
- To reduce pollution - especially air pollution - improve access to clean water, sanitation and healthcare so that fewer die from preventable causes.

*Accessible Cities:*
- To plan cities that provide better public transport services and to create more walkable areas which are accessible for all.

*Intelligent Cities:*
- To use data, connectivity and analytics more effectively to make buildings, infrastructure and citizens smarter and cities more efficient.

**In addition, three emerging concerns are being debated in a number of locations:**

*Safe Cities:*
- Whether it is to prevent terrorism, defend against infrastructure-focused cyber-attacks or deal with increased crime, the need for citizens to feel safe is becoming more pervasive.

*Resilient Cities:*
- The imperative to reconfigure infrastructures that are able to withstand the likely impact of climate change and the increasing number of natural disasters is a growing concern. Adaptation is currently the priority over longer-term mitigation.

*Collaborative Co-opetition:*
- Managing partnership and competition to establish the right balance between sharing experience, insights and ideas for the future while recognizing increasing economic competition between locations.

# Preface

These days the number of mega-cities (those with populations over 10m) is growing across the globe. By 2030 there will be around 40 and 9% of us will live in one.[2] The established conurbations of the 20th century such as New York, London and Tokyo have already been joined by New Delhi, Istanbul, Mumbai, Shanghai and Sao Paulo and by 2050 we will probably add Karachi, Lagos, Jakarta and Dubai to name but a few. Expect their success or failure to become a key area of government and regulatory focus.

**Cities grow because they are a focus for opportunity. As dynamic centres of commerce, cultural eclecticism and knowledge, they are magnets for all walks of life,** frequently attracting the best minds, the ambitious, the brave, the optimistic but also the desperate.

Often cities have gained status in their respective regions as safe havens for those escaping persecution and war, or among those simply seeking a new and better life. The eclectic mix of cultures that results is, in part, responsible for the consequent plethora of transformational ideas, novel technologies, and new ways of doing business, from London to New York, Istanbul to Hong Kong. Despite the media focus on international migration as a driver for change in the last forty years; large scale, internal, rural-urban relocation has also been a powerful engine behind the growth of many cities, particularly across Asia, Africa and Latin America.

But urban population growth is bringing new challenges even as we try and cope with the more traditional concerns around jobs and education. Increasing migration has driven change in living patterns, living spaces and home-ownership models as growing demand and limited supply makes housing prohibitively expensive. It's not just the sheer numbers of people needing a home that drives up land and property values, sometimes regulation designed for different times, such as limits on the height and density of buildings, or constraints on development, can also inflate prices and force workers towards cheaper, but often less productive, locations. Changing these regulatory conditions could make a material difference not only to economies but also to general wellbeing. One study, for example, suggests that in America alone, lifting all the barriers to urban growth could raise the country's GDP by between 6.5% and 13.5%, or by between \$1trillion and \$2trillion.[3] It is difficult to think of many other single policy initiatives that would yield anything similar.

While many benefit from the productivity of cities and the 85% of global GDP that they currently generate, a third of the world's urban population live in unplanned ghettos, townships and favelas. Cities are often polluted, pricey, over-congested and housing everyone is an increasingly major headache – both in the West just as much as everywhere else. London's most populous borough, Islington, has a peak population density of 13,890/km2. This may seem cramped but, when compared to Kamathipura in Mumbai, where there are over 120,000 people per square km, it looks decidedly spacious.

Further, as city populations and densities grow, so too does the pressure on ageing urban infrastructures and the environment. More people in cities means greater need for localised travel, for example. Overstretched transport systems need to be updated in an efficient and sustainable manner. Simply allowing an increasing number of vehicles in confined spaces has meant that air pollution has become a significant health issue across the globe from London and Los Angeles to Delhi and Beijing.

The prospect of flooding is also causing concern. The majority of major cities are built on the coast, or on a river, so rising ocean temperatures caused by climate change are an increasing threat to infrastructure. All of this before we even start thinking about jobs, education and healthcare.

It is clear that many cities are under growing pressure. How can we ensure they evolve in a way that enhances the quality of life for those who live in them? How will we provide for a more socially balanced society? How can we make cities resilient to the challenges of climate change? Is there a better approach to efficient and more collaborative living? And in what ways can cities best embrace innovation and new technologies such as smart data, to help meet the challenges?

Over the past decade or so, we have seen a burgeoning of interest in the challenge and opportunity from city design and development. Many universities, numerous governments, multiple consultancies and a good number of leading multinationals all have research programmes, innovation centres and investment strategies focused on the topic. Indeed, we know of over 500 recent reports covering a wide range of urban issues, and there will be many more.

Most agree that **the problems, albeit differently constituted, are clear, but the complexity of urban development defies simple solutions.** Given this, the Future Agenda Future of Cities discussions were robust, challenging and lengthy.[4]

This document provides an overview of what we heard. It has three objectives:

1. To reflect the views of informed people from many locations on the future of cities

2. To link these thoughts to the research that has already been carried out; and

3. To prompt further debate on some gaps and issues that seem as yet unresolved.

We hope that it is a useful contribution for all those interested in designing cities for the future and helps to bring together a broader range of global views.

# Common Challenges

Across our discussions a number of issues were raised repeatedly and focused on three significant, inter-related, macro-drivers of change. We see these as the common challenges impacting the majority of the world's cities.

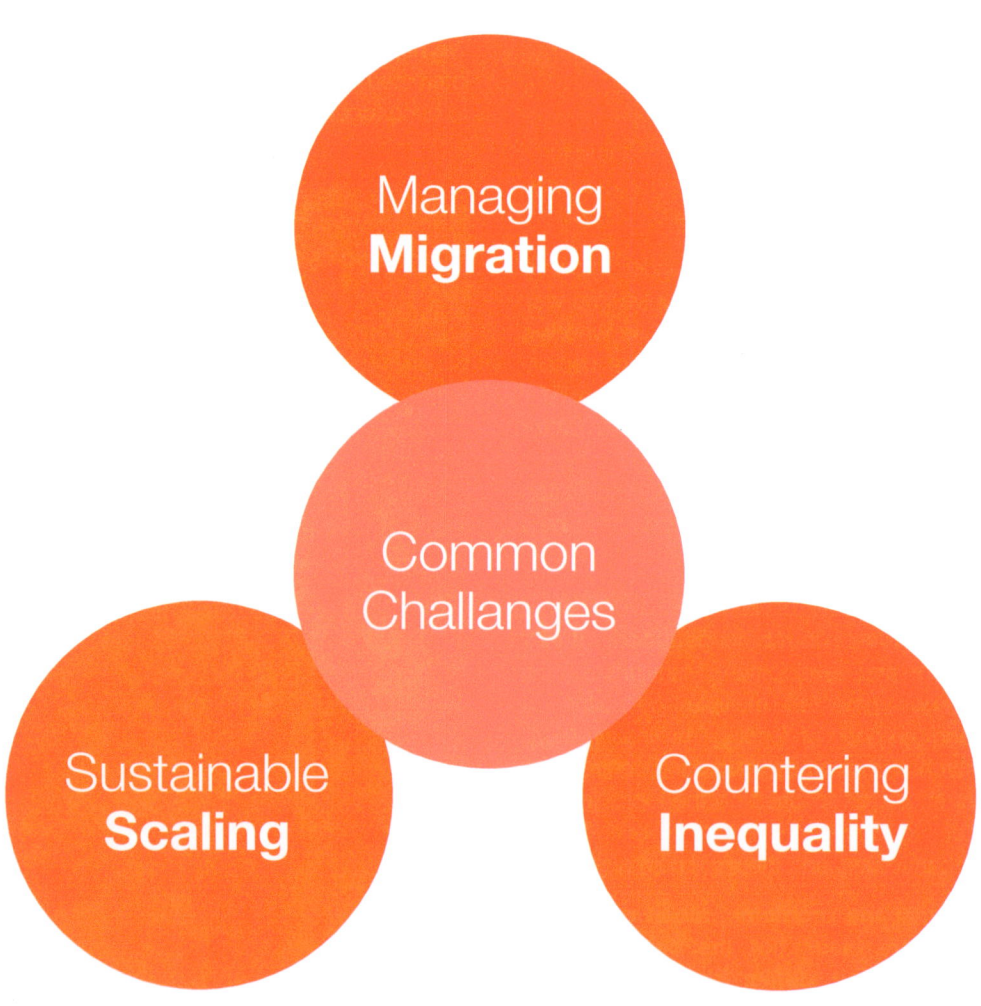

# CHALLENGE 1: Managing Migration

**The facilitation of internal and international migration to cities is set to be one of the defining features of 21st century city management.**

Over the past 30 years, the world's urban population has risen from 1.6 billion to 3.9 billion. In the next 20 years it is expected to surpass 6 billion, with most of the growth now taking place in cities developing countries, those in Africa particularly. Growing migration to cities in most regions is set to be one of the defining shifts taking place for the rest of the century. If managed successfully, accommodating this vast influx of people has the potential to generate huge growth and stimulate an expanding middle class enjoying better living standards; but getting it wrong will set the scene for worsening pollution, urban sprawl, congestion, increasing inequality and rising social tension. Many governments are nervous. Only a few feel able to absorb all new arrivals, many of which may be unplanned and unforeseeable. The majority, it seems, have only limited contingency strategies in place. A key question will be around how urban planners best manage a transition to migration readiness?

**THE URBAN AND RURAL POPULATION OF THE WORLD, 1950-2030**

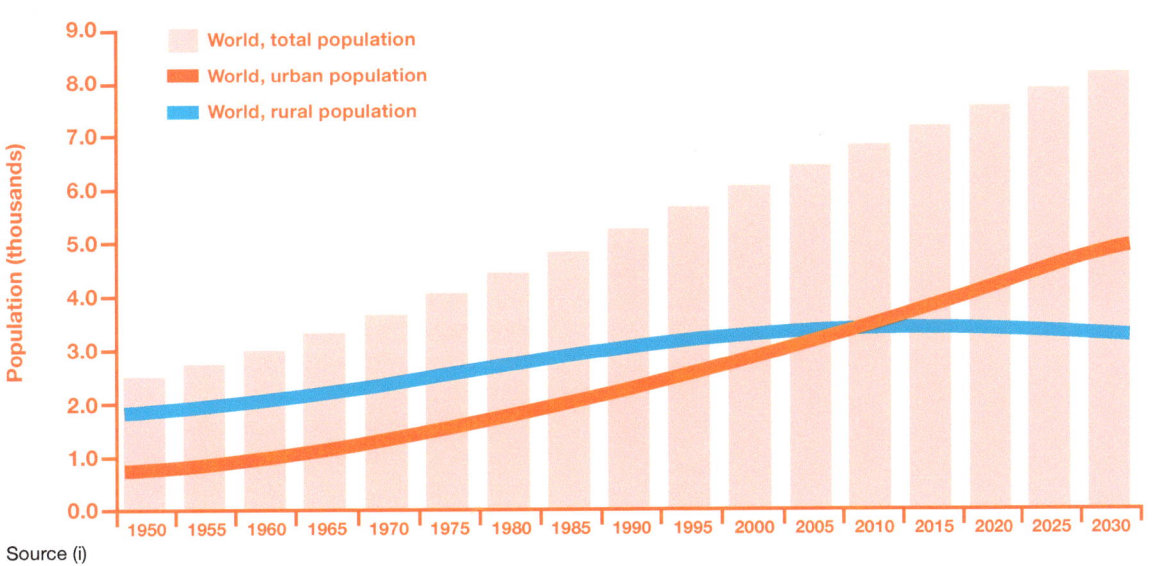

Source (i)

## Pace of Change

According to the LSE Cities research project, around 32 people every hour, day and night, are now moving into Shanghai, 39 into Kinshasa and Jakarta, 42 into Mumbai and Karachi, 50 into Dhaka and 58 into Lagos.[5] This is all pretty much one-way traffic, is happening 24/7 and shows no sign of slowing down. There are many reasons for this ranging from the desire for a better quality of life or the need to flee conflict to escape the impacts of climate change or the desire to find a release from the grinding harshness of rural life.

## Coping Strategies

The scale and pace of this movement is having a huge social, cultural and political impact. Changes that used to take centuries are now occurring in only a few decades, generating huge challenges, including unplanned slums, excessive pollution, destruction of the environment and gaping inequality. Such is the magnitude of these challenges, **some governments have become doubtful of their ability to cope and have tried to either slow the process down or disperse the problem.** As far back as 2013, a UN study[6] of all 193 member-states found that 80% had policies to reduce rural to urban migration. This is more pronounced in poorer countries. 88% of the least developed countries reported they wished to reduce the rate of migration to urban areas.

Given the amount of change underway, many cities are being forced to rethink how they plan their infrastructure and services to cope with fast-rising and yet sometimes statistically invisible populations. Some policies have been designed to slow or halt the rural-urban migration. These range from China's infamous 'hukou' system of residency rights to rural tax and investment incentive schemes in places like Mozambique. Others try to address urban sprawl by, for example, scrapping height restrictions on buildings. One tangible problem is creating enough space for roads: Manhattan is 36% tarmac compared to some unplanned African suburbs where as little as 5% of the land is road. In Saudi Arabia the government has decided to build entirely new super-cities to ease the pressures of the rapid growth of Jeddah and Riyadh, and the Egyptian government is following suit, establishing 20 new cities to divert people away from Cairo. It has plans for 45 more, including a 700 sq. km new capital 'New Cairo'.

In many countries, regulation lags behind urbanisation, which often means that basic services, like schools, transportation, public spaces and land rights, are not being properly delivered to the millions of people living in informal urban settlements, in part because of the speed of urban growth. Although the ambition is to plan for a better infrastructure, many urban leaders are taking too long to do so, which means that by the time a plan has been agreed, large-scale immigration and the consequent muddle of rambling, informal development has already taken place.

**Success in Parts**

Some countries have been more successful. China for example, in an attempt to accommodate the rush to the cities, has spent 8.5% of its national income on infrastructure each year for the last 35 years, far more than Europe and America (2.6%) or India (3.9%). Yet even there, many cities still cannot cope with the speed of urban development which has, quite literally, supersized them, seemingly overnight. Many of them were large already, and now more than 100 have populations exceeding one million.

China also has true "megacities", those whose populations exceed 10m. Of the 30 cities worldwide that match this definition, it boasts six: Shanghai (23m), Beijing (19.5m), Chongqing (13m), Guangzhou (12m), Shenzhen (11m) and Tianjin (11m). A further ten contain 5 to 10m people. At least one of these, Wuhan, will pass 10m within a decade. In addition, 3,500 new urban areas are planned in the next few years. Massive spending on infrastructure has hugely improved connections. But congestion is appalling, air pollution a real health hazard and perhaps more importantly in the Chinese context, residents are complaining. To address this in April 2017 the Central Committee and State Council announced plans for a completely new city, Xiongan, 100 km SW of Beijing. Planned to be three times the size of New York this will be designated a Special Economic Zone and is intended to be a model for future urban design, placing particular emphasis on innovative development, ecological protection and improving people's well-being.

Turning to Latin America, a UN-Habitat report suggests that the urban transition, as traditionally conceived, is almost complete. Despite paying a significant social, economic and environmental cost for this, today almost 80% of the South American population live in a city and there are high hopes that they will experience a "new cycle of urban transition", heralding improved living conditions and a better quality of life. The report argues that, thanks to devolution of planning, local governments now have valuable experience that bodes well for the ability to face the future.[7] The region's 198 large cities - defined as having populations of 200,000 or more - together contribute over 60% of current GDP. The ten largest cities alone generate half of that output. Looking ahead, the McKinsey Global Institute estimates that this is expected to grow to 65% over the next 15 years. This is equivalent to around 6% of projected global GDP growth, more than 1.5 times the contribution expected from large cities in Western Europe, and closer to the growth contribution anticipated from India's large cities.

The African subcontinent faces different challenges. It is the only region where urbanization does not correlate with poverty reduction. For the last two decades' urban growth has been around 3.5% a year. In part, this was caused by migration but looking ahead natural demographic growth due to higher birth rates and lower childhood mortality is expected by some to double by 2050 and quadruple by 2100, and is likely to make an increasingly significant economic contribution. To date, planners have done little to accommodate the influx. According to UN–Habitat 61.7% of urban Africans in sub Saharan Africa live in a slum where only 40% of residents have access to a proper toilet, a figure which has not changed since 1990. In Nairobi, around two thirds of the population occupy 6% of the land. The relative prosperity in North African countries is mainly attributed to better urban development strategies, including investment in infrastructure and in upgrading urban settlements. But bad planning means that, overall, many cities are growing unsustainably faster in size than in population. Lagos, the capital of Nigeria, is typical: it doubled in population between 1990 and 2010 but tripled in area.

**Between 1980 and 2010, the population of S.E. Asia's cities grew at an unprecedented scale** - by around one billion. United Nations projections suggest they will add another billion by 2040. Recent economic successes have lifted hundreds of millions of people out of poverty and created a rapidly growing urban middle class that now numbers almost 2 billion people. Nevertheless, it is also home to the world's largest urban slum populations and the largest concentrations of people living below the poverty line

## International Migration

Much of this growth can be attributed to rural to urban migration but international migration is also on the rise. Together Asian and Middle East cities added more international immigrants than either Europe or North America between 2000 and 2015. Many are often relatively localised as migrants often still want to remain in touch with their origins, keeping a common language for example For instance, the World Bank estimates that 1.5 million migrants from Burkina Faso live in the Ivory Coast - that makes Burkinabe immigrants more numerous than Indians in Britain or Turks in Germany. In India there are more immigrants from Bangladesh than there are Mexicans in America.

Contrary to many media reports, and with the important exception of many European nations and the US, the general public is more likely to be in favour of migration than against it, according to findings of an IOM-Gallup report.[8] However in much of the West, the fear of an influx of low-skilled workers has become an increasingly contentious, even hostile, political issue. Voters in host countries often perceive migrants as a threat to their livelihoods and living standards. Many in the US are, for example, wary of incomers and there is fierce debate raging whether migrants hold down the wages of native workers. In Britain this argument is also made, but alongside this there is added popular discourse around migrants putting pressure on public services, particularly the nationalised health service. Although shown by many experts to be, at the very least, debatable, this is what many in the UK firmly believe to be true.

## Positive Migration

Elsewhere, public attitudes to migration are more sympathetic. When we ran our Beirut workshops in 2016, the inflow of refugees from Syria to Lebanon had just passed 1.5m. Added to the 500,000 Palestinian refugees already in the country, that made a migrant population of 2m in a total of only 6m by the middle of 2016 - there was 1 refugee for every 2 Lebanese nationals. This put into context the 2015 European resistance to 1m refugees being absorbed by a population of 500m. Yet, Beirut does not seem to be distracted from its core focus on growth and development and is steadfastly seeking to follow a master plan to complete the rejuvenation of its Central District and makes the city better for all.[9]

In truth, while concerns around cultural dilution, instability and crime intensify populist agendas, for nations with naturally declining domestic populations (primarily in Europe and the US), there is really no long-term option but to support the economic immigration lever. Certainly, many who participated in the Future Agenda discussions see migration not only as a 'gap-filling' force in the short term but also a foundation for sustained future growth. They also suggested that increasing cultural diversity brings understanding and so makes nations more influential on the world stage. This is supported by the OECD view which states that migrants contribute to labour-market flexibility, pay more in taxes than they receive in benefits, boost the working age population, bring in new skills, add to human capital and fill importance niches in new and old sectors.[10]

# CHALLENGE 2: Countering Inequality

**Providing equitable access to all elements of urban life including transport, sanitation, healthcare, education and work to facilitate economic growth and cement social stability.**

"While cities are powerful engines of opportunity, innovation, and progress, they are also home to growing concentrations of poverty and vulnerability."
– Carrie Thompson, USAID, 2016.[11]

Although economic globalization has created great wealth, it is increasingly clear that its benefits are very unevenly distributed. Affluence has accumulated at the very top of the income scale while the wages paid for service and manufacturing jobs have stagnated or declined.[12,13] Increasingly, we are beginning to understand the harms that this does to society, and yet it seems to have become an almost inevitable part of the story of development. **With more people moving to cities, so widening differences in access to housing, transport, sanitation, healthcare, education and jobs continue to extend the gap between rich and poor.** And although migrant communities may suffer most, urban inequality is rising independent of the numbers of new arrivals.

The GINI coefficient, the most commonly used measure of inequality, shows that some of the areas of highest inequality are the mega-cites.[14] A coefficient of zero equates to perfect equality while one of 100% represents maximum inequality. The cities of Rio de Janeiro, Bangkok and Sao Paulo all have coefficients over 50%. Not far behind in the rankings come Moscow, Shanghai, New York, Mexico City, Los Angeles and London. South Africa is the most unequal country with a GINI coefficient over 60%.

Over the past few decades' inequality between countries has also become an issue. In 2002 Americans were, on average, nine times richer than Latin Americans, 72 times richer than sub-Saharan Africans, and 80 times richer than south Asians.

## CITIES WITH HIGHEST GINI COEFFIENTS

| | | | | | |
|---|---|---|---|---|---|
| 1. | Salvador | 65% | 9. | St Petersburg | 48% |
| 2. | Rio de Janeiro | 62% | 10. | New York | 47% |
| 3. | Sao Paulo | 55% | 11. | Mexico City | 46% |
| 4. | Bangkok | 54% | 12. | Los Angeles | 45% |
| 5. | Bogota | 53% | 13. | Shanghai | 44% |
| 6. | Santiago | 52% | 14. | Chicago | 44% |
| 7. | Moscow | 50% | 15. | London | 44% |
| 8. | Tbilisi | 49% | | | |

Source (ii)

## How Much is Enough?

The key question is how much inequality society can accommodate. Many believe we are at a tipping point, with organisations such as the World Economic Forum suggesting it now poses a material risk to the continued strength of the global economy. Clearly more could be done to address the problem.

In terms of urban development, spatial design has a significant role to play. To date many urban projects, large and small, have contributed to the physical reinforcement of inequality; the proliferation of gated communities is a very good example, as is the scarcity of basic infrastructure in poorer districts. Looking ahead, planners need to include integrated design as a way to assimilate poorer communities into wider city life without compromising the ongoing development of the city.

Inequality is not only about money; more importantly perhaps it is also about access to services such as health and education. Poor access to education, for example, has been identified as being one of the main limits to social development. As LSE's Professor Ricky Burdett recently pointed out, "If one takes education levels of the population in different parts of the city, the quality of education utterly correlates with the availability of, and accessibility to, transit facilities, whether a subway, bus, rapid transit system, or bicycle network. In other words, the better the infrastructure, the higher the educational levels. It is fundamental to remember that decisions made about whether to invest in one form of public transport over another have an impact on the way our children and grandchildren are educated."[15] An efficient, safe and affordable transport system that enables people to easily get to school or to work is therefore a vital component of social integration. A successful example of this can be seen in Bogotá which now has the highest literacy rate in Latin America, in part because its transport policies have taken the locations of public schools into account.

## A Rich Country Problem Too

Urban inequality is not simply a developing world problem. The United States ranks poorly compared to other advanced economies when it comes to income inequality and social mobility. **Across the Americas the United States has one of the highest rates of child poverty** and comes second only to Brazil in terms of the percentage of children living in poor households. As well as having the largest number of millionaires in the country, New York City also has neighbourhoods such as Harlem and the Bronx where average incomes are well below the official poverty threshold. The decline in manufacturing, the legacy of racial segregation policies and the over concentration of the poor in central urban areas are all partially to blame for this.

## The Influence/Need Gap

Although many Future Agenda discussions focus on those living below the poverty line, in Singapore it was highlighted that **governments are often made up of the wealthy elite, many of whom are out of touch with wider societal needs.** This can be exacerbated by the extent of influence the wealthy are able to extend over government policy including those concerned with planning and shaping cities.[16] The power of wealth is evident across many industries of course, some of which impact city planning and development. A 2015 Oxfam report noted that 20% of the world's 1,645 billionaires have interests in the financial and insurance sectors, a group which spends millions on lobbying policymakers in Washington and Brussels and on political campaign contributions, and which saw its cash wealth increase by 11% in the 12 months to March 2014.[17] Some see that this sort of overt influence is unfair and undermines the democratic process; others are more sanguine believing that the overt power of the rich has always been part and parcel of life. They suggest that people in general care less about inequality than they do about economic opportunity, so the focus should be on avoiding stagnation, particularly of the middle classes, and not curbing the excesses of the very rich. The real question, of course, is whether we can actually ignore the rich, or whether in accommodating them, or leaving them be, we are actually prevented from catering for the poor.

### Attracting the Highly Skilled

**Attracting highly skilled workers to a city often leads to improvement in local amenities,** such as the quality of schools, and cultural and entertainment opportunities. Theoretically this has the potential to benefit both the rich and the poor. However, often when an area becomes more attractive, more people want to live there and this has a knock-on impact on the availability and affordability of housing supply. Affordable accommodation can sometimes become beyond the reach of low skilled workers. Even those who have, relatively speaking, well-paid jobs can become 'priced out' and so many up-and-coming cities risk becoming islands for the rich, and too expensive for the poor. Key workers such as carers, cleaners and policemen are obliged to move away, while those who need to, and are prepared to, work in city centres, often face a long and arduous commute.

Cities need workers at all levels, not just the professional elites. Concerns are growing about how to rebalance the situation, with many planners exploring measures to stop high house prices driving a working-class exodus from urban areas.[18] In London a recent report by the University of Westminster and Dolphin Living found that providing subsidised rental homes to key workers resulted in a benefit to the capital's economy of £27,000 per household, not just through their spending power but their wider contribution to the economy, which far exceeds the salary they take home. To cite one example, a nurse will treat thousands of patients a year, getting them back to health and into the workplace.[19]

**Bringing highly skilled workers to an area is not enough to guarantee high wages in a city; the right firms must come too.** Knowledge intensive industries such as technology and finance thrive on the clustering of workers who share ideas and expertise. The economies and populations of metropolises like London, New York and San Francisco have flourished because of this. Success often attracts success; so wealthy cities typically attract multiple high profile, high paying firms such as Apple and Google in London or Microsoft in Beijing. Successful companies pay more, so their workers have more to spend on their homes and in their local community. Some cities are more attractive than others in this regard; McKinsey identifies just 32 which it expects will generate one-quarter of the $23 trillion in urban consumption growth projected from 2015 to 2030.[20]

Without concentrated action, rising inequality will continue to have a destabilising impact on many societies, and especially on urban areas. Inequality narrows the tax base from which municipalities raise the revenues needed to provide essential public services. It also weakens the collective political will to make social and infrastructure investments. What's more, it makes it even more expensive to be poor by limiting access to services and raising the price of private-sector goods and services. To take one example, without access to the mains supply, many living in poverty are obliged to drink bottled water at over 100 times the cost of tap water.[21] In this way, the problems of inequality are compounded.

In the US the decline in manufacturing, the legacy of racial segregation policies and the over concentration of the poor in central urban areas are all partially to blame for increased rates of poverty.[22] Furthermore, the low-skilled, but good-wage jobs on factory lines that many used to climb out of poverty in the 20th century have largely disappeared. The question of how to offer opportunities to those who currently have none, will be one of the defining challenges of the next several decades.

**Joined-up Resources**

Given the inter-relationships between financial inequality and unequal access to transport, healthcare, and education, it is clear that **urban policy has to be increasingly integrated across multiple silos and, in most cities, this demands a far greater level of joined up action than has occurred in the recent past.**

**As income inequality has risen sharply so the need to design a fairer city has become more pressing.** An increase in social housing alongside limiting population density and creating better public spaces can make a difference, as will providing wider access to basic services such as banking, education and healthcare.[23] Mixed-income redevelopment in high poverty neighborhoods, along with the movement of poor people out of concentrated public housing will also help. But to what extent, some ask, can we engineer a more balanced society primarily from a planning perspective and how much will it be driven by a wider collection of actions?

# CHALLENGE 3: Sustainable Scaling

**Ensuring the sustainable development of infrastructure, the reduction of pollution and the creation of a safe, healthy environment in a time of accelerated urban expansion.**

As the urban population and long-term de-densification trends continue, **the area of the planet covered by urban settlements will increase to more than 3 million sq. km between 2010 and 2050.**[24] Globally, never before have we seen such fast scaling of urban environments. If we are to avoid replicating the errors of LA, Las Vegas, Houston, Mexico City and their like, then cities must be planned sustainably.

Most cities are messy sprawling places extending almost endlessly outwards. Even those we consider successful, such as Melbourne or Vienna are buckling under pressure to accommodate the sheer volume of people moving in and the problems that this entails: pollution, congestion and social cohesion, for example. Addressing these is, or should be, a priority.

For some with natural physical boundaries such as Mumbai and Manila, the implication of this is a relentless rise in population density; for others like Cairo, São Paulo and Karachi, unencumbered by physical constraints, the risk is of relentless urban sprawl. It's not just the number of people, changes in living patterns and family and household composition mean that the size of households in most countries is now decreasing putting further strain on housing stock. Partly because of this, many cities are growing faster in size than in population.

It is perhaps in Africa where, with its fast rising population and ongoing shift to city living, that the challenge of sustainable scaling is most significant. It is the world's fastest urbanising continent. **In 1950, sub-Saharan Africa had no cities with populations of more than 1m. Today, it has around 50.** The fastest growing metropolises, such as Nairobi, are expanding at rates of more than 4% per year compared to the average global urban population growth rate of 1.84% a year.[25] Looking at specific cities the numbers can be eye watering. Antananarivo, capital of Madagascar is growing at 5.1% a year while Abuja and Port Harcourt in Nigeria are ticking along at 6.2% and 5.1% respectively. Ouagadougo, capital of Burkina Faso, is experiencing population growth of 7.2% while Mbouda in Cameroon is the continent's fastest growing city at 7.8% annually. Unsurprisingly governments are finding it difficult to provide residents with even the most basic services of housing, water supply, sewerage and solid waste disposal.

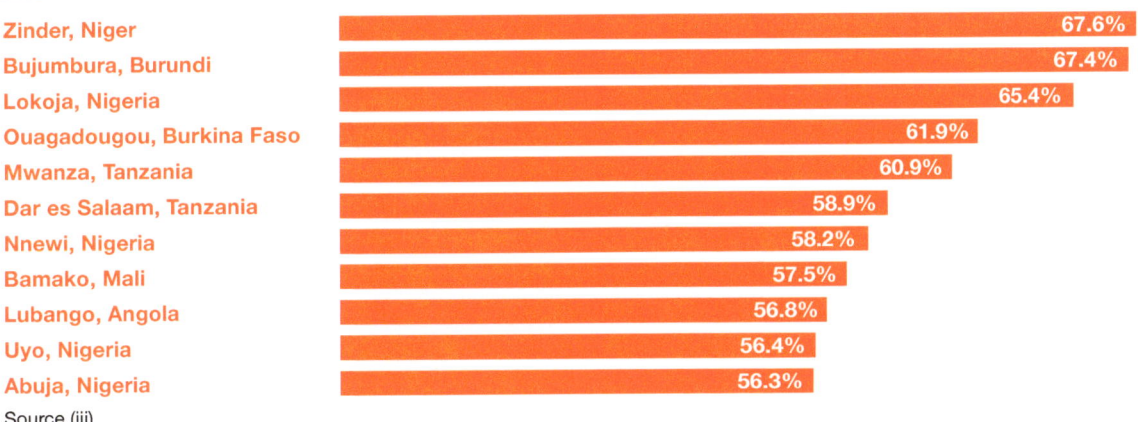

**FASTING GROWING CITIES. Estimated Urban Growth 2016 to 2025**

| City | Growth |
|---|---|
| Zinder, Niger | 67.6% |
| Bujumbura, Burundi | 67.4% |
| Lokoja, Nigeria | 65.4% |
| Ouagadougou, Burkina Faso | 61.9% |
| Mwanza, Tanzania | 60.9% |
| Dar es Salaam, Tanzania | 58.9% |
| Nnewi, Nigeria | 58.2% |
| Bamako, Mali | 57.5% |
| Lubango, Angola | 56.8% |
| Uyo, Nigeria | 56.4% |
| Abuja, Nigeria | 56.3% |

Source (iii)

The core problem is that these metropolises are spreading indiscriminately. In Africa land ownership is often made up of a patchwork of smallholders, so developments emerge wherever a deal can be made. In the jumbled districts that result, far too little space is set aside for roads, parks and other "liveable" amenities. Even middle-class districts often lack sewers and mains water. No one even mentions public parks. Inevitably this will have consequences. Shlomo Angel of New York University has studied seven African cities in detail: Accra, Addis Ababa, Arusha, Ibadan, Johannesburg, Lagos and Luanda. He calculates that only 16% of the land in new residential areas developed since 1990 has been set aside for roads - about half as much as planners think ideal. Worse, 44% of those roads are less than four metres wide. For governments, retrofitting will be difficult, expensive and time consuming. There is hope however, urban authorities in centres like Narok and Kisumu in Kenya, and Moshi in Tanzania are beginning to make positive changes and are investing in improved risk assessments and urban upgrading as well as smarter land use, as the potential for future problems is better understood.

Ideally today's fast-growing cities need to establish expansion areas that can accommodate growth, make space for arterial roads and public spaces, and secure the rights for both. Effective use of expansion area planning would allow for changes in the way streets can be built and the necessary infrastructure installed. The model should be simple, efficient and flexible, attractive to residents and simultaneously economically competitive. **Experts point to densely populated cities like Paris and Hong Kong as the potential blueprints for sustainable living,** rather than the distributed sprawls of Los Angeles and Mexico City. After all, dense living creates efficiencies - Hong Kong uses around 5% of its GDP to move people and goods around; in LA the figure is over 40%.

Given several of the metropolises in Asia and the Middle East are effectively being built from scratch, the opportunity exists to get scaling right from the start. But time is of the essence, as many are expanding faster than planners can draw up the necessary designs. For example, a city such as Dubai, which some expect to grow from 4m in 2016 towards a population of 20m or even 30m over the next 30 years, risks suffering long term challenges as a result of piecemeal development. Unlike the thriving city-state of Singapore, it does not seem to have a comprehensive master plan that can ensure the creation of sustainable communities for example. Without it, Dubai's developers risk creating just another longitudinal urban sprawl that spreads along the coast to Abu Dhabi.

In some locations, such as Cairo and Seoul, we see what has been described as over-urbanisation – they are cities whose rate of urbanization outpaces their industrial growth and economic development. Mitigating against this elsewhere is a common aspiration. Different approaches are being taken at a planning level. For instance, **in many regions establishing satellite cities and networks of 'midi-cities' is seen as a preferred route to more singular mega-city development.** Connected by fast infrastructure, these can act collectively but in a sustainable manner.

"Satellite cities differ from suburbs, subdivisions, and bedroom communities in that they have municipal governments distinct from that of the core metropolis and employment bases sufficient to support their resident populations." – Kai Larsen, Citylab, 2012.[26]

In China, the network model is in full sway. In South East China high-speed trains and super-fast broadband are used to connect a number of smaller cities and create a more coherent centre of population of about 40m. Nine cities including Guangzhou, Shenzhen, as well as the smaller Zhaoqing, Foshan and Dongguan are now gaining from mutual cooperation but without simply morphing into continuous urban sprawl across the whole of the Pearl River Delta.

Irrespective of whether it's extending a market town or a mega-city, there is a call for clear leadership and an integrated approach to link economic development, social change and healthcare, with better transport, access to open spaces and sustainable housing. Often seen as best in class here are Amsterdam's Structural Vision,[27] the Singapore Urban Redevelopment Authority's Master Plan[28] and the London Plan.[29]

**MAP OF SE CHINA CITIES NETWORK**

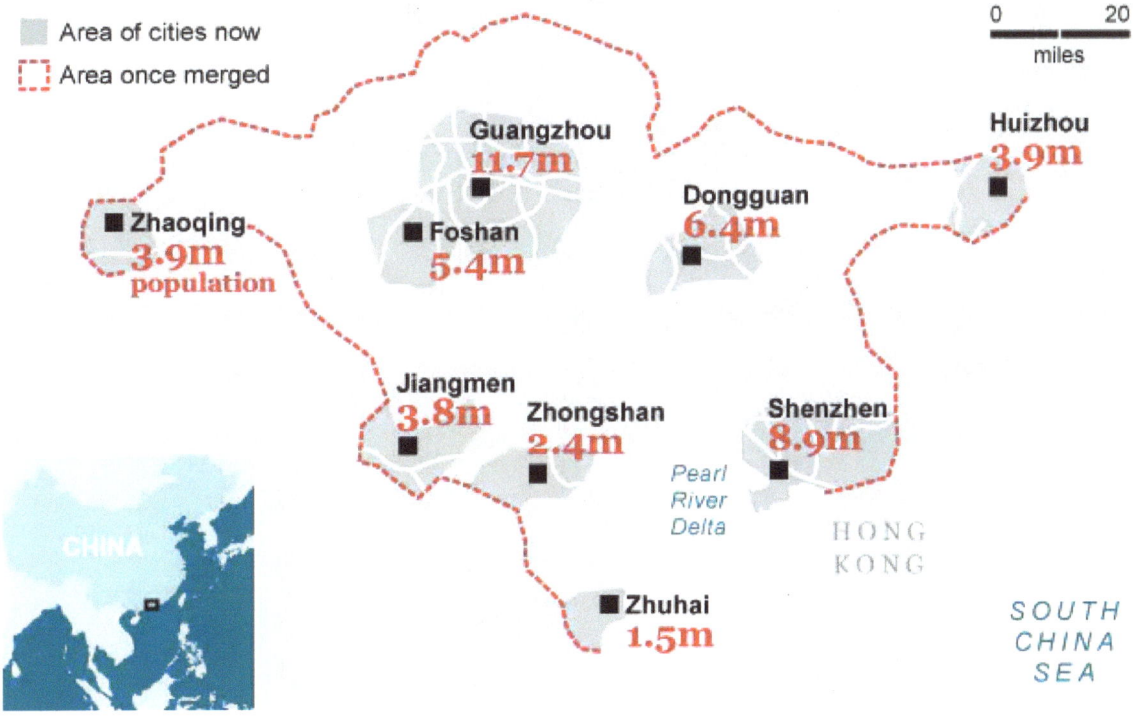

Source (iv)

## Shared Ambitions

Given these common challenges, many urban leaders around the world have similar ambitions for improvement. Everyone wants cities that are healthier, more accessible and which take advantage of emerging technologies to inherently become more intelligent. These issues are not mutually exclusive and addressing the connections between them is pivotal in creating a better urban future.

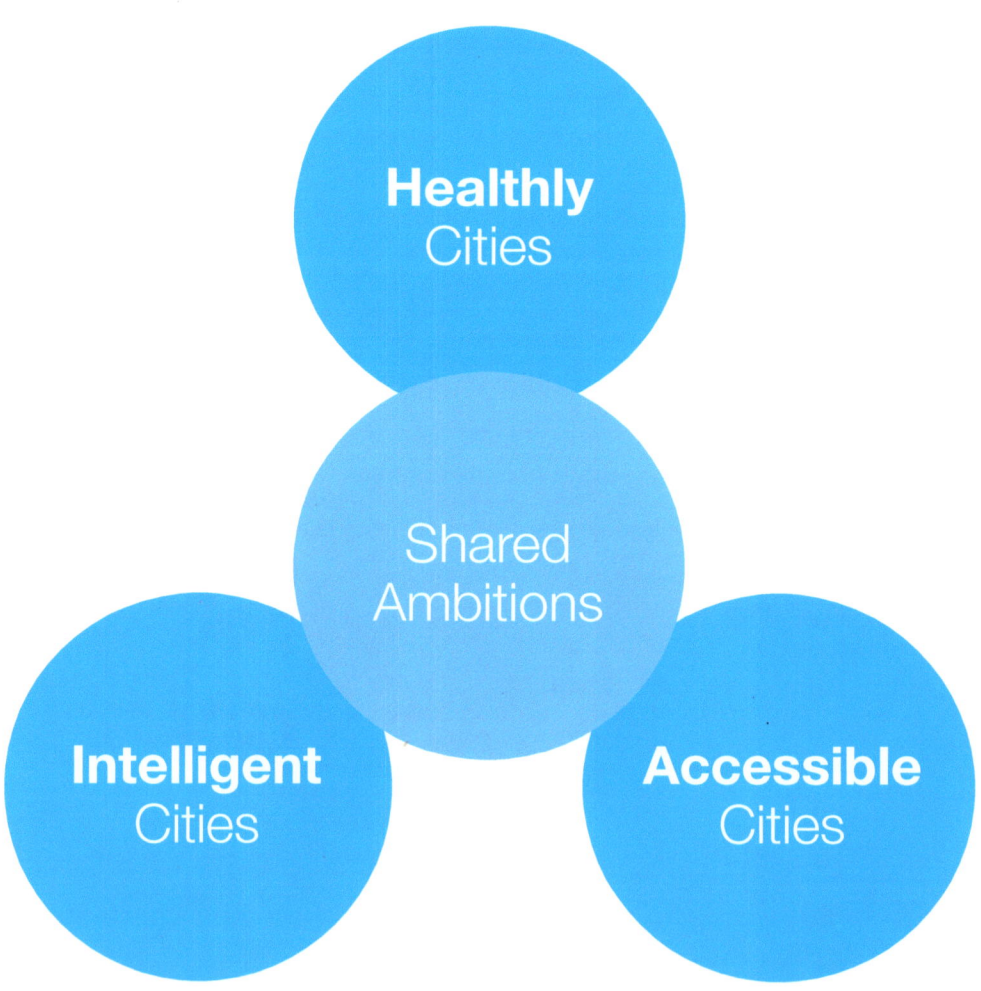

# AMBITION 1: Healthy Cities

**To reduce pollution - especially air pollution - improve access to food, clean water, sanitation and healthcare so that fewer die from preventable causes.**

Whether from polluted air, water, poor waste management or simply a lack of open spaces, the list of unhealthy cities is rising steadily. However, while the problems are obvious, and many solutions are available, the speed at which change can be delivered is a worry. A number of leading metropolises are now individually and collectively seeking to set new standards and so ensure momentum builds, but questions are being raised about how widespread the necessary transformations will be, and what impact can be achieved.

Perhaps **the most detectible threat to healthy cities today is that of declining air quality.**[30] This issue was raised in every Future Agenda discussion. In Mumbai, Delhi, London and Dubai, air pollution generated from within the city is clearly the major concern. In Singapore, it was pollution flowing over the border from forest fires in Indonesia, which on occasion has blanketed the whole island in haze.[31] Even in relatively clean Guayaquil and Beirut, future concerns around dealing with increasing air pollution were also shared.

## 20 WORST CITIES FOR AIR POLLUTION

|    | City | Country | Annual mean, ug/m3 | |
|----|------|---------|--------------------|---|
|    |      |         | PM2.5 | PM10 |
| 1  | Zabol | Iran | 217 | 527 |
| 2  | Gwalior | India | 176 | 329 |
| 3  | Allahabad | India | 170 | 317 |
| 4  | Riyadh | Saudi Arabia | 156 | 368 |
| 5  | Al Jubail | Saudi Arabia | 152 | 359 |
| 6  | Patna | India | 149 | 167 |
| 7  | Raipur | India | 144 | 268 |
| 8  | Bamenda | Cameroon | 132 | 141 |
| 9  | Xingtai | China | 128 | 193 |
| 10 | Baoding | China | 126 | 190 |
| 11 | Delhi | India | 122 | 229 |
| 12 | Ludhiana | India | 122 | 228 |
| 13 | Dammam | Saudi Arabia | 121 | 286 |
| 14 | Shijiazhuang | China | 121 | 305 |
| 15 | Kanpur | India | 115 | 215 |
| 16 | Khanna | India | 114 | 213 |
| 17 | Firozabad | India | 113 | 212 |
| 18 | Lucknow | India | 113 | 211 |
| 19 | Handan | China | 112 | 169 |
| 20 | Peshawar | Pakistan | 111 | 540 |

Source (v)

Although Beijing has the worst reputation, its visible smog is formed mostly from 10-micron particulates that are marginally less deadly than the smaller 2.5 particulates found in much greater concentrations in Delhi. In fact **Delhi's air is 15 times more polluted than the WHO safe maximum.** Whether from vehicle emissions, industrial smokestacks or paraffin stoves, this pollution is manifested across many Indian cities in escalating asthma rates, higher cancer incidence and more heart attacks and strokes. About 620,000 people are dying in India every year from pollution-related diseases.

That doesn't mean it is safer to live in a Chinese city. Air pollution there kills about 4,000 people every day - about 17% of all deaths. 80% of the population are exposed to pollution above safe levels so perhaps it is unsurprising that lives in many Chinese cities are over 5 years shorter than the national average. Indeed, it is said that **the air in Beijing is so polluted that breathing it does as much damage to the lungs as smoking 40 cigarettes a day.**[32] A consequence of this is that the omnipresent paper facemasks of recent years are being replaced by heavy-duty alternatives; parents are even delaying having children because of the poor-quality air.

Richer regions should not be complacent. In Europe over 460,000 people a year die prematurely because of air pollution.[33] In London a 2016 study by researchers at King's College suggested it shortens the city's inhabitants' lives by nine to 16 months. According to the World Bank, when measured across whole nations, some of the most toxic air today is found not in India or China but in the UAE.

Aside from the avoidable deaths and illness, air pollution affects the bottom line. A recent Economist article points to research carried out in the University of California that established a correlation between productivity and air pollution. Three call centres in China were monitored and it was found that workers were around 6% more productive on low-pollution days than on days when pollution was high.[34] When you consider that the Chinese service sector, much of which takes place in city offices, now accounts for over half the country's GDP then the impact on this across the economy is huge. A reduction in China's air pollution index by just 10 points could boost worker output by at least 15 billion Yuan ($2.2 billion) per year.

**C40 Action**

Some cities are successfully battling against bad air. **Led by the mayors of C40 cities such as Paris, Madrid, Athens and Mexico City there is now a concerted effort underway to reduce emissions.**[35] Both by introducing bans for diesel vehicles and creating incentives for electric vehicles by 2025, they aim to change the market. Also by pedestrianizing large sections of their city centres and promoting walking or cycling, their ambition is to change citizen behaviours, encouraging them to leave their cars behind. It hasn't all been plain sailing; poorly thought-through policies that cut carbon emissions sometimes also cause a rise in other air pollutants, such as SO2 and NOx. Most notably, over the last decade fuel-tax policy in Europe has incentivised drivers to switch from petrol cars to diesel ones, cutting carbon-dioxide emissions but increasing these from NOx and particulates

Perhaps one of the boldest moves in recent years has been in California where the Environmental Protection Agency has been behind the adoption of a mandate for Zero Emission Vehicles (ZEV). The programme's objective is to ensure that automakers research, develop, and market electric vehicles.[36] This is a gradually scaling regulatory requirement for carmakers to switch from internal combustion engine (ICE) products with production volumes steadily ramping up by 2025, when about one out every seven cars sold must be ZEVs. In Delhi an experiment to reduce car emissions by restricting road use to odd- or even-numbered license plates on alternate days (a method occasionally used in Beijing, São Paulo and a dozen other cities) seems to have been an initial success.

### Eco Civilisation

However, potentially the most significant action on a global scale is China's Eco-Civilization initiative.[37] Poorly covered by Western media but repeatedly mentioned in our workshops in Beijing and Shanghai, this is an unprecedented massive switch of China's economy to be carbon neutral by 2030. Implicit within this is not only the end of the internal combustion engine and the scaling down of coal power, but also significant fines and regulations for industrial polluters. A directive of the Chinese Communist Party, many see this as a game-changer. As a Trump-led US signals a potential retreat from some global climate agreements, many see that with the Eco-Civilization initiative and other international commitments, **China will take the lead on climate change and reducing urban air pollution and so set the standards for others.**

### Polluted Water

Although neither as visible nor as widespread an issue, **the availability of clean water is another major challenge to healthy city living.** Untreated or poorly treated sewage can be low in dissolved oxygen and high in pollutants such as faecal coliform bacteria, nitrates, phosphorus, chemicals, and other bacteria. Treated sewage can still be high in nitrates. Groundwater and surface water can be contaminated from many sources such as garbage dumps, toxic waste and chemical storage and use areas, leaking fuel storage tanks, and intentional dumping of hazardous substances.[38] As populations grow and climate change increases it stands to reason that the likelihood of drought, water rationing in cities is also likely to rise.[39] From Baku in Azerbaijan and Dzerzhinsk in Russia to La Oroya in Peru, Tianying in China and Vapi in India as well as multiple African cities such as Dar es Salaam, Luanda, Ndjamena and Brazzaville, the inventory of the world's most polluted cities includes many suffering from water contamination.[40]

In our water discussions in Brisbane, experts highlighted that many of the solutions lie not only in cleaning up water supplies but also in encouraging industry and citizens to use more recycled water. With Singapore's Newater as the exemplar,[41] even in a water scarce environment, simple joined up actions can transform the water supply and massively reduce contamination.

## Waste Management

Add on to air and water the issue of poor waste management and the list of the most polluted cities expands still further. Dhaka, Delhi and Portau-Prince are three of the most well-known, but cities such as Moscow also make the cut.[42] Lagos, with a population of 21m or so, spews out 10,000 metric tonnes of waste a day only 40% of which is collected at all and of that only 13% of recyclable materials is salvaged from the city's landfills. Other cities face different waste challenges: When we ran the workshops in Beirut, for purely political reasons the garbage had not been collected for six months. In our travels, the most visible location for effective waste recycling was Vienna, but globally the standard bearers for minimum landfill include Switzerland and San Francisco: the former due to behavioural compliance with regulations and the latter because of technology adopted in waste processing.

Given that many cities have neither the regulation in place nor can afford the technology, the question is often raised about how others can achieve similar success. In Mumbai and Nairobi there is a deeply embedded cultural norm around minimizing waste and so a lot of informal recycling – there is value in what is thrown away. People pick through rubbish at dumps looking for items such as plastic bottles that can be sold to recycling factories. But still, there are many enormous waste dumps within ever growing urban boundaries. These heaps contaminate the soil and groundwater. Plastics flow down rivers into the sea, harming ocean life. Without drastic action, some estimates suggest that **there will be more plastic than fish in the world's oceans by 2050** and 99% of seabirds will suffer from ingested plastics.[43]

China's rising consumer class means that its' cities are already running out of good places for landfills so they are turning instead to burning rubbish, and some are putting this to good effect by generating electricity at "waste-to-energy" plants. About 70 such incinerators are now being built. In addition to more than 180 already in operation, this is dramatically increasing the capacity to incinerate waste. Shanghai produces the most household rubbish: around 22,000 tonnes a day.

It is perhaps curious that more cannot be achieved through recycling because some recycled materials could be cheaper than virgin commodities. However, **although recycling can go some way to improving the situation, the lack of closed loop infrastructure and associated technology mean that scope is limited.** Furthermore mismanagement and poor planning means that many countries throw too much stuff away. Much depends on public, political and corporate appetites. Despite the fact that making

cans from recycled aluminium requires 95% less energy and creates 90% less greenhouse-gas emissions than virgin stock more than 40 billion aluminium cans hit America's landfills every year - alongside $11.4 billion worth of recyclable containers and packaging. In part this might explain why America's recycling rate has stalled at around 34% for two decades—far lower than most rich countries.

On a more positive note nearly 50 countries, including the entire European Union, operate a policy called "extended producer responsibility" which shifts the burden of waste disposal from taxpayers to companies. Although by no means perfect, such schemes boost recycling rates and so save cities money by shifting the burden to the corporates. In the US thirty-two states already force companies to handle discarded electronics, batteries, mobile phones and other products and Rhode Island recently introduced a bill that calls on them to recycle at least 80% of packaging by 2020. Some corporates are embracing the need to change. For instance, Coca-Cola has recently announced it supports testing a deposit return service for drinks cans and bottles in Scotland while Pepsi, Nestlé, Unilever and M&S have already committed to producing more eco-friendly bottles by using plant-based materials or less plastic.

It remains the case that people are dying every day because of pollution. The generic solutions are well understood: fewer polluting vehicles; tighter emission controls on industry, improved sewage systems, enforcing regulations on chemical dumping, less use of kerosene for domestic cooking and improved waste management. The challenge is that managing this effectively requires a joined-up combination of secure funding, political will and population behaviour change.

**Urban Obesity**

Beyond dealing with the pollution challenges, many cities are also seeking to encourage their citizens to be more active and overcome another fast growing health threat, that of urban obesity. Mass urbanisation, reduced activity and poor diet are all accelerating its rise. Levels in most cities are growing fast and the associated healthcare burden will soon account for 5% of global GDP.[44] Despite the well understood issues, the problem is getting worse – the World Health Organisation points out that in 1995, there were an estimated 200 million obese adults worldwide and another 18 million under-five children classified as overweight. As of 2000, the number of obese adults had already increased to over 300 million. In 2016 30% of the global population was overweight or obese. This looks set to rise to 50% by 2030.

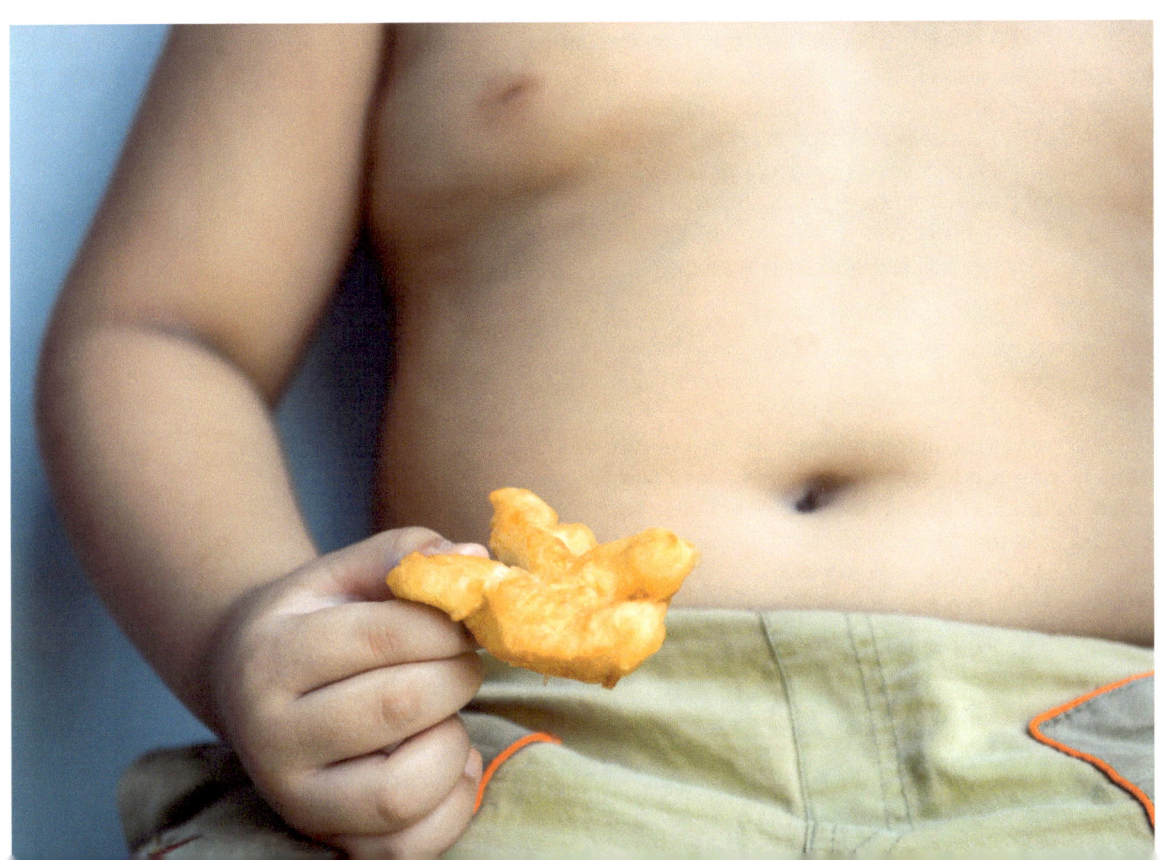

No country has yet reversed the obesity epidemic; quite the contrary. In the UK the average waist size has increased by over an inch in recent decades.[45] In part it is economic forces that are conspiring to cause the great global weight gain. Countries grow wealthier and increase consumption. People move from rural areas to cities, where they have ready access to inexpensive, processed foods and take less exercise. Machines do work that humans once did, also decreasing the amount of energy people use. Moreover, the growth in the global food industry means the reach of junk food has never been greater.

Obesity brings with it all sorts of associated illnesses. In India research has shown that **migration from rural to urban areas is directly associated with an increase in abdominal obesity,** which in turn drives other health risk factor changes such as insulin resistance, diabetes, high blood pressure, and dyslipidaemia. Indeed, the rates of obesity and diabetes are more than double in urban Indians than their rural counterparts. Across Africa, the issue of rising urban obesity, especially for the poor, is also evident. In urban Kenya, Senegal and Ghana it is running at twice the level found in rural areas. Given that it has a higher incidence in disadvantaged households, it also imposes a disproportionate burden on the poor in terms of healthcare costs. Again, the solutions of better diet and more exercise are well known but getting sufficient traction is a problem for most public health authorities.

With obesity trends intertwined with economic forces, some advocates say that health considerations need to be written into trade and economic policies. Certainly **urban planning has a role to play in obesity prevention by, for example, designing cities to encourage more outdoor activity.** We can observe that several governments are being pressured to ensure that public spaces are created and retained. There is rising public support for the creation and maintenance of public parks and destroying them is increasingly unpopular. As was seen in Istanbul in 2013, many public demonstrations against the potential development of Gezi Park sought to change government policy.[46] Going forward all those we talked to saw that environments that reconnect people with each other and their city brings multiple benefits including increased healthier citizens, better community engagement and improved mobility.

Some cities have already adopted a "health in all policies" approach. Seinäjoki, a community in Finland, has seen positive results using this strategy. Six years ago, nearly 1 in 5 five-year-olds were overweight or obese in this city. As a result of implementing their obesity prevention plan this number has been reduced by 50 percent. Focusing on the school environment in particular, the community works together to improve child health. This comprises physical and nutrition education, including cooking classes and yearly health exams for all students. This success story underscores the point that it is possible to halt the obesity epidemic. The challenge is that currently few other societies act together in as coherent a manner as the Finns.

### Agreed Benefits

If we chose to measure successful cities not by their output but by the longevity and happiness of their inhabitants then some argue there would be a greater incentive to plan for a healthier environment to drive real change. No new technologies are required. **Policies encouraging a healthier lifestyle will improve urban design** and consequently result in reduced pressure on healthcare, better community resilience, and overall offer improved life expectancy. It is largely about acting on what we already know. Governments, schools, media, businesses, health care providers, families and individuals all need to play important roles in promoting healthy lifestyles and creating a climate for sustained change.

# AMBITION 2: Accessible Cities

**To plan cities that provide better public transport services and to create more walkable areas which are accessible for all.**

**People Not Cars**

We live in a world where the majority of our cities have been designed for cars first and people second. Whether you look at an aerial photograph of Shanghai, Dubai, LA, or pretty much any US urban area, what you see is a highway-focused environment. Equally, on the streets of Mumbai, Cairo or Jakarta you encounter roads that are bursting with vehicles well beyond their design capacity. Some think that in the US and Europe we have reached peak car but everywhere else the growth of the car shows little sign of slowing anytime soon. Cities will bear the brunt of this, making them increasingly unhealthy, dangerous and polluted.

**Many believe that urban life could be better without cars – or certainly without so many of them.** City planners have known this for years but now they are, at last, doing something about it. Oslo, for example, has announced that it will ban all private cars from its city centre by 2019 and Dublin and Milan also have similar intentions. Helsinki has ambitious plans to make its "mobility on demand" service so good that nobody will want to drive a car in the centre by 2025, while Paris's car-free days have successfully reduced high pollution. New cities – such as the Great City[47] on the outskirts of Chengdu, China, and Masdar[48] near Abu Dhabi – also plan to focus on mass transit or electric cars.

**Walking or riding a bike is certainly healthier and generally safer. Public transport is frequently cheaper.** Copenhagen and Amsterdam, where 70% of mobility is either by walking or cycling, are recognised leaders in supporting non-motorised transport. Even Los Angeles recently announced plans for hundreds of miles of bus and cycle lanes. Oslo plans to build at least 40 miles of new bike lanes, introduce rush-hour charges (on top of existing congestion fees) and remove parking spaces

From Guangzhou and Brussels to Abu Dhabi and Chicago, cities are shifting their attention from keeping cars moving to making it easier to walk, cycle and play on the streets. Speed limits are being slashed, some central roads are being converted into pedestrian promenades and others flanked with cycle lanes. More than 700 cities in 50 countries now have bike-share schemes. Bogota in Colombia captured the imagination as far back as 2000 when it introduced Ciclovía, or 'cycle only Sundays'. Now adopted by approaching 100 cities in over 20 countries it is just one example of imaginative initiatives that are bringing people back onto the streets.

One solution is simply to make cars slow down. Slower traffic makes neighbourhoods quieter and safer. Speed bumps, pedestrian countdown lights and slow zones around schools mean that New York now has fewer deaths each year than when it started counting them in 1910. Sweden has halved road deaths since 2000, and cut them by four fifths since 1970. London recently cut the speed limit to 20mph on more than 280km of its roads and is getting rid of pedestrian-unfriendly giant roundabouts. Toronto has reduced the speed of traffic on more than 300km of its roads.

**Poor Public Transport**

And yet these initiatives are still the exception. For most conurbations today, the future threatens to be one with more cars, albeit increasingly electric and autonomous. The lack of good public transport, coupled with rising incomes in some places, has pushed up the use of cars. Pew Research estimates that in Lebanon, where the only public transport available is by bus, 81% of Lebanese households have a car. It is no wonder Beirut's roads are busy.

Meanwhile in other, poorer countries where cars are still too expensive for many, donkeys and carts, tuk-

tuks and matatus fight for space in shantytowns. All this adds to the congestion, the noise and the delay. A World Bank study estimated (conservatively) that 4% of Egypt's GDP was lost each year because of time wasted in traffic in Cairo. It also makes city streets very dangerous. In the developing world, laws and safety measures are failing to keep up with population growth, urbanisation and rising car use. Ironically by paying for new roads that are not safe, development banks and donors can sometimes make it worse. A quarter of the pupils at the Nesco School in Kibera, Kenya's largest slum, were involved in a road crash in 2016 because they have to cross multi-lane highways on the way to classrooms. A safe crossing would have made all the difference.[49]

**Better Public Transport**

What can be done to sort this out? A good public transport system would be a start. It certainly makes a city more accessible and efficient. Munich, Singapore and even London have led the way in reinvigorating their wider use. Indeed, with its population doubling, **Singapore sees mass transit as a core driver for a more effective city.** By 2030, 80% of households will be within a 10-minute walk of a train station and 75% of journeys will be on public systems. In Medellin, in Colombia, the government increasingly collaborates with business to improve the institutional fabric as well as core infrastructure through building new cable cars and metros. In many of our future of transport discussions, the issue of providing cities with better public transport systems, and particularly the use of multi-modal hubs to enable easy access between one transport option and another was raised repeatedly.

**CITY POPULATIONS IN WALKING DISTANCE OF RAIL AND METRO STATIONS**

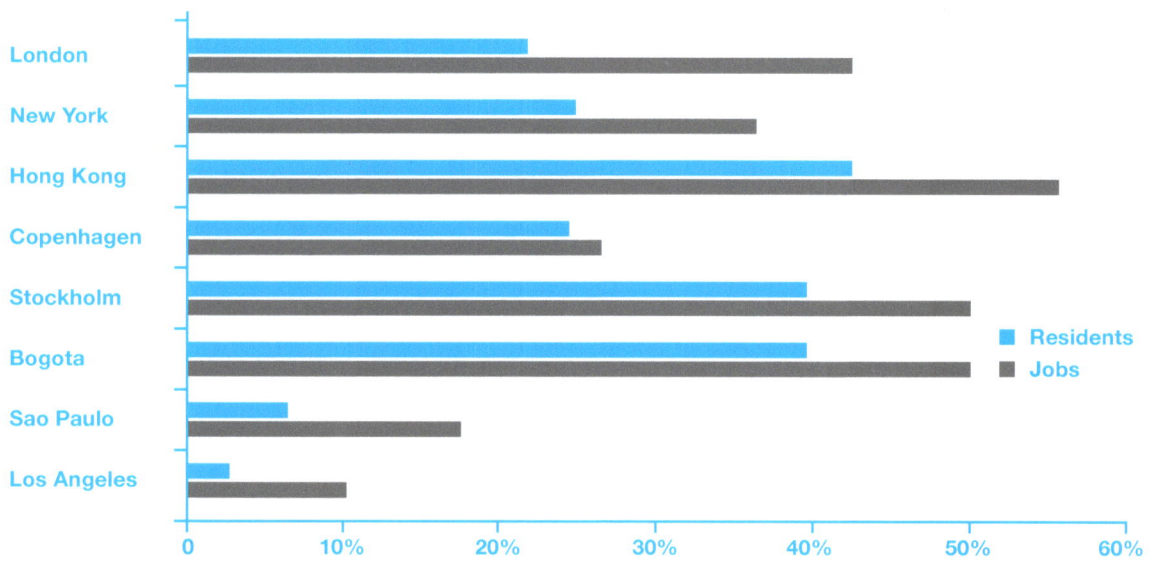

**The proportion of metropolitan residents and jobs within 500 metres (5 to 10 minutes' walk) of rail, metro and bus rapid transit stations.**

Source (vi)

But shiny buses and trains are not always enough to tempt people out of their cars. Sometimes a nudge is also needed. Governments, from Egypt to Iran, have started to remove fuel subsidies, causing the price of petrol to rise. Road tolls and higher parking charges are also effective tools. Led by London's example, congestion charges have dramatically reduced the number of cars in many cities. Beyond this, technology is also transforming the public transport experience as smart phones allow you to use apps to check routes and pay for trips. In Helsinki, residents will soon be able to travel within the city by using an app that mixes and matches a variety of public and private means of transport. If there is no obvious route, a bicycle from the city's bike share programme or a walking alternative will also be suggested. Several such schemes in other cities are due to start this year.

### Walkable Cities

In their comprehensive 2016 report, Cities Alive - Towards a Walking World,[50] engineering firm Arup have done a good job in highlighting some of the multiple challenges, opportunities, benefits and design options for creating more accessible cities and noted the impact of such issues as spatial quality, car and bike sharing. The report points out that **walkable cities are safer, more attractive, more inclusive and easier to govern.**

The High-Line in New York, the Cheonggyecheon River in Seoul,[51] the Eixample area of Barcelona and more recently Beijing's historic Hutongs district are all good examples of significant, high profile developments which have transformed the walkability of cities. But small tweaks make a difference too. In London as long ago as 2004 Mayor Ken Livingstone vowed to make the centre "walkable". The changes he suggested included a scheme to create clearly marked maps for use across the city. Most boroughs now have the distinctive yellow-branded signs on their streets allowing people to better understand the distance between tube stops; for example, from Covent Garden to Leicester Square is only 0.3m (0.5km). This means more people choose to walk. Streets are also being adapted to be more pedestrian-friendly. In South Kensington, chock-a-block with tourist friendly museums and cafes, the removal of curbs and the replacement of tarmac by granite bricks to create a more prominent shared use space has meant that fewer cars choose to go down the main Exhibition Road, providing more space and a safer environment for pedestrians.

### Local Clusters

As well as providing better public transport and more open walkways, compact spaces are made more appealing to those with a focus on health, environment and sustainability. To achieve this the idea of local hubs for those working in knowledge-based or specialist sectors, has long been proposed as a means of minimising the daily commute to a few hundred metres at the maximum. 'Work, live, play' clusters in cities allow residents to access different activities all embedded in one area. This point was highlighted equally in Singapore, London and Dubai. However, with many people currently spending up to 4 hours a day travelling between home and work, achieving this is not so simple, requiring a change of mind set around the ways businesses operate. Yet as organisations become more flexible, porous and virtual, as was outlined in our discussions on the Future of Work, the necessity to be in the office every day may recede.

Implicit in this, as was first raised in our New Zealand discussions, is the importance of improving digital connectivity enabling people to work more effectively from home or in local communities rather than having to commute into offices. Enhancing the speed and reach of broadband is a fundamental in achieving this objective.

**Cities for Ageing Populations**

Many see the need to make better accommodation for the elderly in an urban environment, especially, in developed countries where 80% of older people are expected to live in cities by 2050. Arup's Shaping Aging Cities report[52] reinforces the point that they "will need to change, to make sure older people continue to play an active role in the community and don't become isolated. Isolation has a negative impact on health so tackling that is really important." In terms of solutions, again simple changes can make a significant difference: "Reducing the distance between transport stops, shops, benches, trees for shade, public toilets and improving pavements and allowing more time to cross the road all encourage older people to go out."

Some consider that improving building access, more assisted living schemes and adopting more US style retirement communities are part of the solution. Others push back against this and advocate "integration rather than segregation" and support the opportunity for people to "live independently as long as possible." The solution is probably a combination of the two – giving those who can, the opportunity to remain in their own homes and those who are more vulnerable, the security of community living.

Learning from Japan, the country with the highest dependency ratio of all, **some see examples of governments prioritizing more age-friendly cities.** The principle of the compact / dense city is again highlighted where "people live in limited residential areas close to services and with good public transport – so they don't need to drive." Key here is not to characterise ageing as a problem but to recognise that these strategies make life better for everyone as well as helping older people.[53]

**Increasing Accessibility**

Moving forward, the cities without extensive public transport systems should focus on improving access to other forms of transport without constraining the broader movement of people and goods by vehicles. Creating pockets of walkable spaces is evidently possible in many locations but interconnecting these effectively to make fully walkable cities seems to be the greater challenge. The cable car approach taken in Medellin, which is surrounded by hills, was often quoted in our discussions as a low cost but effective people mover for this city and hence one option for others. Most agree that in many cities **there should be more innovation focus on better, low-cost systems that can affect greater movement of people and things in a more effective way.** If densely populated Hong Kong only uses 5% of its GDP to move people and goods around while widely spread LA uses over 40%, there is clearly a major efficiency gap. While cities cannot be re-built, better thinking about multi-modal transport options and encouraging different, more effective solutions is a must for many.

# AMBITION 3: Intelligent Cities

**To use data, connectivity and analytics more effectively to make buildings, infrastructure and citizens smarter and cities more efficient.**

### The Smart City Ideal

Increasingly equipped with digital technologies and 'big data' **many cities are now making buildings, infrastructure and even citizens smarter** and therefore making themselves more "intelligent". In the main it's down to technology. "Bossy tech" - technology that intervenes - is the new big thing in many mayors' offices from London to Boston, Quito to Delhi. City planners are keen to take advantage of the improved connectivity by creating more sensors and using fast-developing analytics to interpret them. In Barcelona, as just one example, this use of technology is adding resolution both in terms of greater detail to what is already known and also making connections which were previously unknowable. Data from multiple sources across the city can be transmitted and analysed in real time so that lights can be switched off, heating monitored and rubbish bins emptied - all without the help of a human hand.

Source (vii)

The information and knowledge gathered by multiple devices and integrated with real-time monitoring systems is used to tackle inefficiency – reduce queues at train stations, ensure the traffic runs smoothly, help ambulances get to accidents and the police to crime scenes. Collectively, many see that smart data can deliver a world where renewable energy systems, effective transport networks, and digital infrastructures all align to create a super-efficient and more sustainable urban environment.[54] IT companies, industrial conglomerates, governments, transport organisations and a plethora of start-ups recognise this potential and are keen to build on the opportunity.

As bossy tech gets bossier and public authorities become used to the notion that, at the click of a button, human behaviour can not only be monitored but changed, the truly intelligent cities will be the ones which can combine the corporate compulsion for efficiency with the human desire for privacy, security and community.

**Smart City India**

It's easier to deploy new systems where there is new development. Here India and China have arguably greater opportunities than many. India has already invested $15bn to create 100 smart-cities as satellite towns. The aim is to improve basic infrastructure, water, sanitation, power supplies and public transport, and to significantly enhance IT connectivity thereby providing 'smart' solutions to the urban challenges. The first, GIFT City, is being built on 886 acres (358 hectares) of semi-desert near Ahmedabad, in Gujarat. Despite the fact that it is an earthquake zone, the hope is that the new metro, 25,000 new apartments, hospital and artificial lake will attract high-profile companies and eventually generate around a million jobs – mainly in the financial sector. Certainly the state owned banks have already signed up.

Although the smart city concept may well be refined to include existing cities, locations for all the 100 new smart cities in India have been tentatively named and states will experiment with plans for them, bidding for central funds for their development ($945m was budgeted for 2015).

In China, by contrast, much focus to date has been placed on accelerating development in one city, Yinchuan, ahead of others. This is where smart payments, buses, taxis, rubbish bins and lockers plus holographic receptionists are already part of the mix. The government has created a joint venture between the city and the private sector – namely ZTE, the Chinese multinational telecom company. As principle and technology are proven in the test bed of Yinchuan, already tagged by CNN as 'the smartest city on earth' then they will be quickly deployed into 200 more smart city projects across the country.[55]

## Corporate Partnerships

Several other notable examples have also turned to municipal / corporate partnerships to help deliver the dream. IBM's Smarter Cities / Smarter Planet initiative has been embraced by mayors in cities such as Rio de Janeiro where massive sensor networks, cloud-based storage and predictive analytics have all been integrated. Intel has installed sensors all over San Jose to measure air and water pollution, noise, traffic flow, energy usage, communication, and public transportation use. In addition to producing efficiencies, the programme has created over 25,000 local jobs in clean technology as an added boon. Although behind schedule, Masdar in the UAE is still aiming to be one of the most sustainable, environmental and smart cities on the planet; and Songdo in Korea has implemented Cisco's 'Smart+Connected' view of the city.

## The Voice of Caution

Some temper their corporate and technology enthusiasm with a little pragmatic realism. Author of an often-mentioned book on Smart Cities, Anthony Townsend, points out that the smart city is not a seamless web of integrated and joined-up technologies and probably never will be.[56] Rather, he argues, it is more an opportunity to match the right pieces information to the circumstance and individuals and so make our environment more liveable, functional and equitable through the use of new technologies. Indeed, **smart cities could be just as much about better governance and urban planning than about integrated machines.** "Smart cities need to be efficient but also preserve opportunities for spontaneity, serendipity, and sociability. If we program all of the randomness out, we'll have turned them from rich, living organisms into dull mechanical automatons."[57]

Others are even more reserved about total interconnectivity and suggest the vast network of sensors amount to millions of electronic ears, eyes and noses – so future cities will be transformed into places of perfect and permanent surveillance by whoever has access to the data feeds. They point to Rio De Janiero as a precursor of this. Townsend writes: "What began as a tool to predict rain and manage flood response morphed into a high-precision control panel for the entire city." He quotes Rio's mayor, Eduardo Paes, as boasting: "The operations centre allows us to have people looking into every corner of the city, 24 hours a day, seven days a week."[58] Not everyone is comfortable with this.

## Smartphone Impact

Whether urban areas should be left to be intelligent in themselves or whether technology should enable citizens to be more informed, take better decisions and so participate more actively, is often debated. Certainly, assuming universal connectivity, digital platforms such as **smartphones have the potential to bring people together and collaborate to 'fix' problems and so create a more efficient system.** They allow us to interact with and better understand our environments. Pivotal here is presenting people with accurate information at the right time to prompt them to make positive decisions – be that on activity, diet, destination or mode of travel. If the right prompts are given at the appropriate moment via the most effective medium, often an app, then whether choosing A over B or deciding to do C can sometimes become easier. However, there are already constant demands on our decision making capabilities, not least from commercial advertisers so it would be wrong to assume that everyone will be able or will want to participate in every decision-making opportunity.

## Open Data

Six years ago the US became the first country to make all data collected by its government "open by default" - except for personal information and that related to national security. Almost 200,000 datasets from 170 organisations have been posted on the data.gov website. Nearly 70 other countries have also made their data available: mostly rich, well governed ones, but also a few that are not. Open Knowledge, a London-based group, reckons that over 1m datasets have been published on open data portals using its CKAN software, developed in 2010. There are many beneficiaries of this, from individuals checking out traffic routing, to councils deciding on upgrading road links, to businesses looking for suitable sites for a new restaurant in a high footfall area.

**Once information is free and open, then different parties and interests can start to collaborate.** In the US, the urban open data movement has been growing for several years, with cities including New York, San Francisco, Chicago, and Washington leading the way. Bryant's Park in New York was one of the early local hubs for the development of citizen based networks from which sharing has spread. London, which currently has more open public data sets than any other European city, is fast taking a lead in this area. Other UK councils including those in Bristol and Manchester are making the information they hold on city parking, procurement and planning, public toilets and the fire service publically available. In other locations, cities such as Helsinki, Rio, Dubai and Singapore have all opened up significant public data sets and are exploring different options to make good use of them.

## Big Data Analysis

At first, the open data movement was driven by a commitment to transparency and accountability. City, state, and local governments have all released data about their finances and operations in the interest of good government and citizen participation. Companies like OpenGov enable city managers and residents to examine finances, assess police department overtime, and monitor other factors that let them compare their city's performance to neighbouring municipalities.

Perhaps **the most intriguing data sharing and analysis to date has been in Los Angeles with the LAPD.**[59] Using years – and sometimes decades – worth of crime reports and combining this with weather conditions, traffic updates, sports events and retail activities its algorithms analyse the data to identify areas with high current probabilities for certain types of crime. These are then streamed into patrol cars that proactively go to these locations. While some see this as too intrusive and a step towards Minority Report's 'precogs', this is all about predicting where and when crime is most likely to occur, not who will commit it. Performance is already impressive – with police presence in identified locations reducing around 20% of crime events and rising.

What seems clear is that open data, used appropriately can make cities safer, cleaner and more efficient but, to do this, citizens, consciously or not, will live under constant surveillance tracked by sensors, cameras and drones. What is not clear is how secure this data can really be. We know that the openly accessible data of London's cycle hire scheme can be used to track individual cyclists.⁶⁰ This sort of information when in the wrong hands can make individuals and their possessions very vulnerable; consider theft, the tracking of children, wide scale fraud and even terrorist attacks. How can we protect ourselves from unwanted intrusion? To date the privacy debate around this has yet to have much public airing; when it does it may well generate strong feeling for many parties.

**Responsive Cities**

Given what is already technically possible, many are now looking at how far the intelligent connected city can progress. How can we best mix the Internet of Things with the Internet of Bodies⁶¹ to optimise cities? Leading thinkers in the field include Carlo Ratti, Director of MIT's SENSEable City Lab⁶² who we met in Istanbul. He sees that the way we describe and understand cities is being radically transformed and believes that using sensing to better comprehend urban flows is a key step forward. He argues that the **pervasive digital systems that layer some of our cities are already transforming urban life** for some and once this information is better shared between planners, designers and the public then we can collectively shape our future cities.

**Smarter Citizens**

As more digital systems become part of the urban fabric, a new generation of products and services are emerging that make cities more responsive, interacting and adapting with overlapping systems. They are therefore able to respond to citizens more efficiently. Always-on devices connect people to each other, physical space and dynamic processes. As Saskia Sassen of Columbia University notes that it will be vital to "leak the (human) knowledge of the neighbourhood into codified systems – like a backward Wikileaks… and activate the citizenry".⁶³ Top down data collection is mixed with bottom up data aggregation to give more and more interlinked sources of information - 'Big Brother' and 'little sisters' together.⁶⁴ This allows cities to be more responsive, encouraging the direct engagement of citizens in the planning and management of their home and wider community. The ideal is that cities ultimately become adaptive, emotional and experiential environments that are able to connect and process information, and most importantly adapt to the changing needs of the citizen.

# Emerging Concerns

Alongside the common challenges and ambitions discussed, three emerging concerns were raised during our research and are seen as areas where future resource needs to be focused. While not yet applicable to every urban environment, the leading examples highlight that momentum is building.

# CONCERN 1: Safe Cities

**Whether it is to prevent terrorism, defend against infrastructure-focused cyber-attacks or deal with increased crime, the need for citizens to feel safe is accelerating.**

One of the key issues that the Chinese interns we talked to in Dubai saw as important for the future was to live and work in safe cities. While security in Dubai is clearly high, these students felt that achieving similar levels of safety would be important for many other leading cities in the years ahead. Whether to prevent terrorism, provide defence against more infrastructure-focused cyber-attacks or dealing with increased inequality, the need for urban environments to better protect their citizens was highlighted at several events.

## Safest Cities

Taking a holistic view across security from digital, health, infrastructure and personal perspectives, the EIU 2015 Safe Cities Index identifies Tokyo as the world's safest city closely, followed by Singapore.[65] In Asia, Jakarta and Ho Chi Minh City are at the bottom of the list. While wealthy nation cities are generally above average in the rankings, they should not be complacent; Riyadh for example is one high-income city with a low safety index. Here and elsewhere, **gated communities provide a sense of security for those who can afford to live in them.** In Chile, Santiago has seen a significant growth in gated communities over the past decade while, as far back in 2004 Johannesburg had 300 enclosed neighbourhoods and 20 security estates.

| | Total Score | | | Personal Safety | | | Digital Security | |
|---|---|---|---|---|---|---|---|---|
| 1 | Tokyo | 85.63 | 1 | Singapore | 90.42 | 1 | Tokyo | 87.18 |
| 2 | Singapore | 84.61 | 2 | Osaka | 90.2 | 2 | Singapore | 83.85 |
| 3 | Osaka | 82.36 | 3 | Tokyo | 89.31 | 3 | New York | 79.42 |
| 4 | Stockholm | 80.02 | 4 | Stockholm | 87.51 | 4 | Hong Kong | 78.78 |
| 5 | Amsterdam | 79.19 | 5 | Taipei | 85.67 | 5 | Osaka | 77 |
| 6 | Sydney | 78.91 | 6 | Hong Kong | 85.09 | 6 | Los Angeles | 74.99 |
| 7 | Zurich | 78.84 | 7 | Toronto | 84.82 | 7 | Stockholm | 74.82 |
| 8 | Toronto | 78.81 | 8 | Melbourne | 82.72 | 8 | San Francisco | 73.85 |
| 9 | Melbourne | 78.67 | 9 | Amsterdam | 82.39 | 9 | Abu Dhabi | 73.71 |
| 10 | New York | 78.08 | 10 | Sydney | 80.4 | 10 | Chicago | 72.9 |
| 11 | Hong Kong | 77.24 | 11 | Barcelona | 78.36 | 11 | Toronto | 72.04 |
| 12 | San Francisco | 76.63 | 12 | London | 77.35 | 11 | Montreal | 72.04 |
| 13 | Taipei | 76.51 | 13 | Zurich | 76.62 | 13 | Santiago | 70.51 |
| 14 | Montreal | 75.6 | 14 | Doha | 76.41 | 14 | Sydney | 70.48 |
| 15 | Barcelona | 75.16 | 15 | Lima | 74.81 | 15 | Washington DC | 69.99 |
| 16 | Chicago | 74.89 | 16 | Frankfurt | 74.57 | 16 | London | 69.42 |
| 17 | Los Angeles | 74.24 | 17 | Washington DC | 73.95 | 17 | Amsterdam | 68.81 |
| 18 | London | 73.83 | 18 | Istanbul | 73.7 | 18 | Mumbai | 68.07 |
| 19 | Washington DC | 73.37 | 19 | Seoul | 73.62 | 19 | Zurich | 67.04 |
| 20 | Frankfurt | 73.05 | 20 | Mumbai | 73.61 | 20 | Melbourne | 65.42 |
| 21 | Madrid | 72.35 | 21 | San Francisco | 72.96 | 21 | Taipei | 65.11 |
| 22 | Brussels | 71.72 | 22 | Delhi | 72.7 | 22 | Brussels | 64.6 |
| 23 | Paris | 71.21 | 23 | Los Angeles | 71.66 | 23 | Kuwait City | 64.21 |
| 24 | Seoul | 70.9 | 24 | Paris | 71.29 | 24 | Delhi | 63.33 |
| 25 | Abu Dhabi | 69.83 | 25 | Chicago | 71.27 | 25 | Shenzhen | 62.74 |
| 26 | Milan | 69.64 | 26 | Bangkok | 70.97 | 26 | Milan | 62.62 |
| 27 | Rome | 67.13 | 27 | Milan | 70.87 | 27 | Mexico City | 61.69 |
| 28 | Santiago | 66.98 | 28 | New York | 69.45 | 28 | Madrid | 60.78 |
| 29 | Doha | 66.41 | 29 | Montreal | 68.48 | 29 | Barcelona | 60.29 |
| 30 | Shanghai | 65.93 | 30 | Shanghai | 67.66 | 30 | Buenos Aires | 59.58 |

Source (viii)

### Counter Terrorism

Around the world, increased terrorism has become a growing concern for everyone. Recent terrorist attacks in Mumbai, Paris, Brussels, Ankara and London, to cite just a few, are centre-stage for many security forces, urban planners and increasingly the general public. Preventing attacks from happening and minimising their impact when they do is now a priority in many locations. This is made all the more complex because of the changing strategy of assailants, some of whom employ low-tech but extremely effective approaches, such as driving cars into crowds with the intention to cause harm, for maximum effect.

In some cities planners use counter-terrorism architecture such as bollards, barricades, street furniture and open spaces to reduce this risk.[66] The UK's RIBA was one of the first organisations to explore the options and provide design guidance.[67] It highlighted the benefits that can be achieved from using glazed facades, large staircases and enhanced landscaping in public spaces.[68] While extreme approaches, such as those being used within and around the new US Embassy in London, with its seclusion zone, and six inch glass walls, are necessary in some areas, for the majority, more modest, but effective street architecture does, at least, provide a shield.[69] One thing for sure is that **designing for counter-terrorism without turning nations into uninviting fortresses is a delicate balance.**[70]

### Foiling Cyber-Attacks

Although physical attacks and the options to counter them can be highly visible, behind the scenes equally significant changes are taking place to deter and prevent increasingly common cyber-attacks against urban infrastructure. In one of our 2015 future of privacy discussions that involved leading members of the intelligence services, it was stated that the number of cyber-attacks that had been prevented in the UK alone that year was put in the thousands. As the Internet of Things increasingly connects everything from cars to street signs, fridges to supermarket checkouts, our mobile data and health information to distant monitors and so on, the risk of fraud and the possibility of error will become a constant in our lives. While some consider that this will simply become an inevitable part of everyday life, and is similar to the risks we already take when driving a car or getting on a train, others are warier, believing that the new **integrated connectedness makes security management significantly more challenging.**

As was often pointed out, the IT sector and security services may well prevent a thousand attacks (or more) each year, but it only takes one major breach to potentially cause panic. Most vulnerable are the utilities, especially energy supply and water treatment/distribution facilities. Closing down a power grid is seen as the worst-case scenario in much security risk analysis.[71] While Russian hackers have recently taken down the energy system in Ukraine, industry experts see that other nations, including the US are also in danger.[72] As energy systems are evermore interconnected, the ability for hackers to deny citizens supply for months, not just hours, is a real possibility. This is a major worry and security contingencies see that a week of no power in many urban districts could lead to food and water shortages and even civil breakdown. Currently, cities vary widely in terms of how prepared they are for possible attacks.

### Safe Cities

US locations such as New York, Los Angeles, Chicago and San Francisco are all relatively secure digitally but the focus on technology and cyber security does not seem to be matched by success in combating physical crime. All are outside the top 20 for personal safety. London, with one of the most extensive networks of CCTV monitoring of any city, has a camera for every six citizens. And yet, at the time of writing, crime rates in London are rising, some argue because of the reduction of policemen on the beat. Madrid has more than 8,000 security cameras distributed throughout its mass transit system. However, some studies suggest that CCTV does not in fact have an impact on levels of crime and violence. At best its impact is modest.[73]

### Maintaining Social Cohesion

Alongside terrorism and cyber-attacks, the third main security risk that was highlighted was that of social cohesion, especially in a world of rising migration and inequality. **Urban environments can be incubators for crime.** Hot spots generally occur in areas that are characterized by poor social cohesion and control. Addressing this is a priority and so many cities increasingly have plans to combat inequality and improve the quality of life for all citizens. But success is proving elusive. Consider Rio de Janeiro that in 2010 launched Morar Carioca, a high-priority plan to convert its slums, or favelas, into recognized city communities by 2020. Roughly one-fifth of the city's residents — around 232,000 households — live in these favelas, most without basic sanitation, and with little in the way of building standards. Under the 'Municipal Plan for the Integration of Informal Settlements' Rio planned to bring municipal services like clean water and waste collection into the favelas; upgrade urban infrastructure (such as providing energy-efficient lighting); improve residential buildings and more.[74] As a bold initiative the plan won several international awards.[75] However, five years later this ambitious and visionary project was packaged into the Olympic legacy framework, co-opted by political interests, and then abruptly dismantled without much explanation.[76]

Social psychologists treat cohesion as a trait that combines with others in order to influence the way the group does things. Sociologists tend to look at cohesion as a structural issue, measuring how the interlocking parts of the whole group interact to allow it to function. Within cities, providing people with incentives such as fulfilling employment, a good home environment and a sense of self-worth are seen as primary drivers for greater cohesion. Equally important is the principle of social norms – effectively the acceptable behaviour within a society. Norms tend to keep a group working better together as long as everyone acts within the same framework.[77]

Within urban planning, a key design approach to improving cohesion is identifying spatial strategies that can alleviate the concentrations of urban poverty and inequality and provide better access to jobs, housing, education, health, public space, transport and community infrastructure.[78] Green spaces and access to sports facilities, for example, can have a huge positive impact. Medellin in Colombia, site of innumerable gang murders a mere few decades ago is again a good example of how sport can help transform communities beyond recognition. Problem favelas were reintegrated into the city with publicly funded sports facilities and better transport connecting them to the city. Others now taking heed of good examples, are following suit and are seeking to introduce similar more integrated planning policies.

# CONCERN 2: Resilient Cities

**The imperative to reconfigure infrastructures that are able to withstand the likely impact of climate change and the increasing number of natural disasters is a growing concern. Adaptation is currently the priority over longer-term mitigation.**

Resilience reflects a city's ability to persevere in the face of an emergency. In our discussions in both Christchurch and Guayaquil, the need for cities to be more resilient to natural disasters was emphasized above many other issues. In many ways this was no surprise given that both have recent experiences of earthquakes. Christchurch was hit most significantly in 2011 killing 185 people and rendering much of the city centre uninhabitable, while the 2016 earthquake in Ecuador was centred on Manabi Province and killed over 670. Whether from earthquakes, flooding or other acute shocks, in an age of wider climate change recognition, many cities are asking how they can be more robust to withstand and combat the effect of natural disasters and extreme, less predictable weather patterns.

**Climate Change Impact**

**No one really knows exactly what the impact of 2, 3 or 4°C of rise in global temperature will mean** as it is genuinely unchartered territory, but the UK Met Office has created one map of likely consequences of 4oC based on the IPCC Assessment Report. Alongside further melting of the Arctic and Antarctic ice sheets, this shows desertification in the Amazon, South West USA, Southern China and large parts of Africa. In terms of weather, drought and hurricanes will increase in frequency and strength and the seasons will shift. However, the most concerning issue that we need to prepare for seems to be flooding. Whether stemming directly from rising sea levels and more heavy rainfalls or as a by-product of more unstable weather patterns, dealing with more water than our systems were designed to handle is the top climate risk in many urban regions.[79]

Historically many communities were adjacent to water and cities have naturally developed in the same locations. Today most of the largest cities are located on the coast and so are increasingly vulnerable to flooding. New York, Miami and Boston, alongside Guangzhou, Mumbai, Kolkota, Shenzen and Jakarta are among the most vulnerable. The ten most 'at risk cities' globally already have combined populations of over 150m and are projected by the UN to have grown by a further 50% by 2015, adding another 75m.

**Flooded Cities**

**The vast majority of our cities are not prepared for flooding** and yet 22 of the top 50 wealthiest are prone to serious flooding that will impact housing, the poor, cost of energy and social breakdown.[80] By 2070, the total asset exposure could rise more than tenfold from today, reaching $35 trillion, more than 9% of projected annual global economic output. Over the longer term, experts estimate that up to 1 billion people will have to migrate inland or north this century as a consequence of climate change. For the majority, who are simply unable to move, dealing with this will become the biggest priority. Over the past decades, many of us have consistently built where we should not and, in many regions, flood plains have not been respected. Moreover, other than in the Netherlands, few buildings have been designed to accommodate regular flooding. Multinational learning visits to the Netherlands, a sensible idea for planners and decision-makers, are frequent but, as yet, few tangible new projects have been proposed.

**Preparing for Resilience**

**The real opportunity is to rethink infrastructure in terms of resilience, and not just rebuild it.** In only a few cities more effort is being put into building new infrastructure similar to the Thames barrier in London. Designed in the 1960s and operational since 1982, this helps to defend London from high tides and storm surge. Originally intended for use

## WORLDS MOST AT-RISK CITIES FROM FLOODING

| Total Score | | | | | |
|---|---|---|---|---|---|
| 1. | Guangzhou | China | 11. | Jakarta | Indonesia |
| 2. | Mumbai | India | 12. | Abidjan | Ivory Coast |
| 3. | Kolkata | India | 13. | Chennai | India |
| 4. | Guayaquil | Ecuador | 14. | Surat | India |
| 5. | Shenzen | China | 15. | Zhanjiang | China |
| 6. | Miami | US | 16. | Tampa | US |
| 7. | Tianjin | China | 17. | Boston | US |
| 8. | New York | US | 18. | Bangkok | Thailand |
| 9. | Ho Chi Minh City | Vietnam | 19. | Xiamen | China |
| 10. | New Orleans | US | 20. | Nagoya | Japan |

Source (ix)

only once or twice a year, in 2014 it was closed 48 times. This increased frequency both reinforces the need for long-term planning, and acts as a reminder that it is reaching the end of its capacity to protect. Similar sustainable flood-risk management schemes are being discussed and planned for areas like the Pearl River Delta in China where currently the practice is to deliberately flood rural areas in order to protect cities.

No one is expecting migration to vulnerable cities to stop, or for cities to voluntarily relocate any time soon, but with insurance now impossible to obtain for some locations and more regular flooding occurring in others, the need for action to be taken will be increasingly visible over the next decade. If global warming plays out as many expect, attitudes to flooding will shift considerably, good practice will be shared and a there will be a more widespread view around better preparing for resilience.

After the damage from Hurricane Sandy, New York has embraced an approach originally conceived in London that calls for agencies to start adopting resiliency measures immediately, monitor how well they work, and continually update their understanding of climate risk information and responses as the climate system and resilience actions evolve. The report "A Stronger, More Resilient New York" outlines 250 projects to protect the city's coastline, and to strengthen buildings, energy systems, transportation networks, parks, telecommunications, health care operations, and supplies of food and water.[81] Sea levels in the vicinity of New York City are rising at almost twice the global average rate. As much of the city's critical infrastructure is located within the '100-year flood zone' so the core challenge is how to dedicate the resources to adapt and rebuild infrastructure to be able to cope with the expected changes in water levels. While some in Washington DC see that, in the longer term, eventually the whole city may need to relocate, others believe that this can be avoided. Digital technologies may well help to monitor the situation and as cities become more intelligent and responsive it is hoped they can also become more resilient.

New York has gained a lot of focus, however other cities face more immediate threats. As such there is a flurry of collaborative activity underway in order to improve resilience.[82] Most significant here is the 100 Resilient Cities collaboration a network dedicated to helping cities around the world become more resilient to physical, social and economic challenges.[83]

The 100 Resilient Cities network sees that urban resilience is the capacity of individuals, communities, institutions, businesses, and systems within a city to survive, adapt, and grow no matter the kind of chronic stresses and acute shocks they experience. These include high unemployment, inefficient public transport, rising violence as well as food and water shortages - each of which is clearly critical and variously occurring in conurbations around the world. However, given the growing impact of climate change, greater focus is now also being placed on a city's ability to adapt and cope with more acute shocks such as earthquakes, flooding and also more pandemics.

**The City Resilience Framework**

Developed by Arup with support from the Rockefeller Foundation, The City Resilience Framework[84] provides a lens to understand the complexity of cities and the drivers that contribute to their resilience, and a common language that enables cities to share knowledge and experiences. It is one of several examples of joined up thinking taking place that connects the multiplicity of factors that underpin urban resilience.

In some of our discussions it was recognized that, given the climatic shifts now evidently underway, efforts to mitigate climate change are needed but may not have impact any time soon. If preventing more chronic stresses and acute shocks is not possible, then we need to adapt to the changing conditions. Indeed, the language of adaptation and resilience is becoming more commonplace. Globally we can see different cities already pushing differing, more adaptive approaches. For example, Toyko's cap-and-trade program for reducing greenhouse gas emissions, the first for an urban centre, requires large commercial, industrial, and government buildings to cut their carbon pollution via energy efficiency or emissions trading.[85]

**Resilience Efforts**

Led by both city mayors and, significantly, the big insurers such as Swiss Re and Munich Re[86], more proactive efforts to address the impacts of climate change are now taking place. These range from the creation of Chief Resilience Officers[87] who focus, coordinate and lead each city's resiliency efforts to the development of resilience bonds[88] that generate capital for risk reduction projects. How quickly these and other initiatives can scale and have impact ahead of the next acute shock remains to be seen. Several climate change experts consider that many of the implications from global warming for this century are already underway and that the point of no return for temperature rises above 2°C is looming, bringing with it extensive, but unpredictable shifts. The problem is that the changes we make today will only begin to have tangible impacts in the next century. Therefore improving the resilience of key cities to get us through to 2100 intact is no small task.

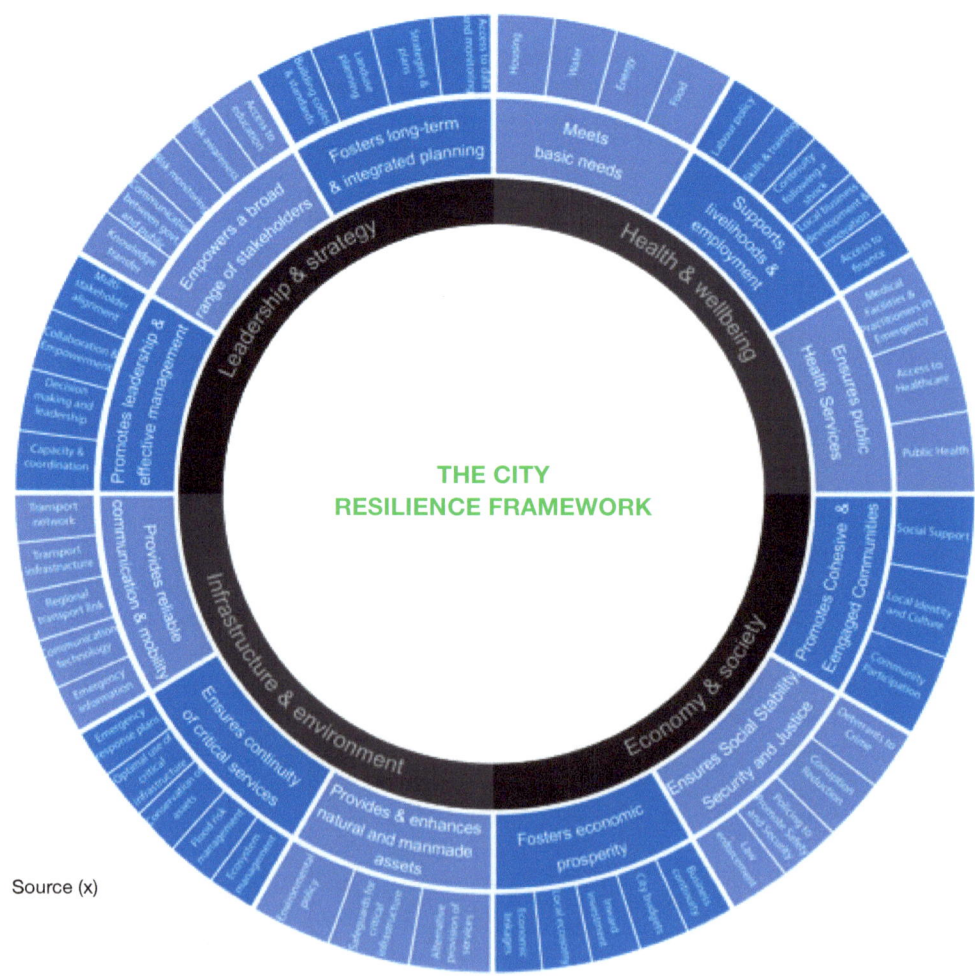

Source (x)

# CONCERN 3: Collaborative Co-opetition

**Managing partnership and competition to establish the right balance between sharing experience, insights and ideas for the future while recognizing increasing economic competition between locations.**

Cities always have and always will compete and compare with each other. But with many shared challenges now being aired, the level of inter-city collaboration taking place is also increasing. 100 Resilient Cities is one example already discussed. The C40, is another great network example that connects policy makers from 83 cities around the world in order to address the impact of climate change and learn from each other about issues such as waste management, building efficiency and transportation. Through efforts like these, cities are taking the lead ahead of national and regional governments in tackling the key issues for the future. However, balancing greater collaboration with the ongoing demand to compete is a tricky balance to maintain.

### Growing Competition

Since the days of Sparta and Athens there has been competition between cities. While the means of gaining competitive advantage may have changed, the continuous battle for leadership has not abated. **The big cities of today and tomorrow operate in a constant state of competition.** They jostle over everything: positioning and attractiveness through to design, innovation and strategic city branding. This competition among metropolises is intense, and a strong city brand has become a potent weapon to maximise its profile allowing it to differentiate itself from its others.

The World Bank sees that a competitive city is one that successfully facilitates its firms and industries to create jobs, raise productivity, and increase the incomes of citizens over time.[89] But culture and liveability also has a role to play. What is increasingly evident is the increasing competition between cities to attract skilled, entrepreneurial people to live and work within them.[90]

### National and International Rivalry

The need to attract high-value, high-wage businesses in services and professionals in the likes of research and design, new technologies, the financial and media industries is seen at both in-country and international levels. Within India, cities such as Mumbai, Pune, Hyderabad, Chennai and Bangalore are all striving against each other to be the national leader in digital business.[91] Across the EU, cities such as Paris, Frankfurt, Amsterdam and Dublin are all positioning themselves to attract more financial services jobs from London particularly following Brexit. Attracting significant FDI (foreign direct investment) has been a hallmark of Singapore's success. The same is true for London, Dublin, Shanghai and New York.[92]

### Quality of Life – A Source of Competition

**New forms of competition are emerging particularly around quality of life and the overall cleanliness, safety and greenness of the urban environment.**[93] Dubai, for example, has emerged as not only a regional, but also a global centre, which invites talent, sprouts imaginative architecture, attracts the headquarters of major global firms and creates competitive infrastructure.[94] But it now also

suffers from serious pollution with air containing 80 micrograms of pollutants per cubic meter. That's slightly higher than China's at 73 micrograms and more than double India's at 32. Unless it can better manage this, its aspiration to attract the brightest and the best might remain just that.

## Collaboration

Many see that today cities must not only compete to succeed they must also collaborate. Through networks, cities find opportunities to undertake joint projects in areas of mutual interest and benefit. **Inter-city collaboration is becoming a priority for any mayor's office.** Sharing, learning and partnering on the big issues for the future are becoming a necessity. Working across multiple sectors and issues, the C40 convenes networks that provide a range of services in support of urban climate change efforts. It has 17 networks organised under 6 initiative areas covering mitigation, adaptation and sustainability topics which are of highest priority to cities at risk of the greatest impact from climate change. They help cities replicate, improve and accelerate climate action. These city-only working groups provide a forum for honest knowledge exchange, enabling cities to tap into the global expertise of their peers as well as providing the connections for technology partnerships. C40 networks also amplify individual city solutions by providing a global platform for showcasing city successes.[95]

Some suggest the role of cities as problem solvers is rising while other government bodies such as nation states are increasingly being considered obsolete or dysfunctional.[96] A key element in this is that cities have more to offer, presenting a greater goodwill, more flexible configuration and a better mind-set for collaboration than national governments. Specifically, a good number of municipal leaders tend to be more resourceful problem solvers. As cities must cope with the practical day-to-day realities, mayors and councils find themselves more obliged to deliver services rapidly and effectively. They are often also more able to test and refine approaches faster than national governments. Equally, local executives usually exhibit a less partisan and more pragmatic style of governance. Indeed, the mayors of many cities show a quality of leadership that encourages collaboration. Some are going further than others: Metropolitan areas like Denver and New York are shunning competition and focusing on how entire regions can work together to reach economic goals.[97]

The C40 and the 100 Resilient Cities are not the only forums. Other collaborative networks of urban organisations and governments are emerging on a regular basis. The World Cities Culture Forum includes a network of 27 cities founded in 2012 that share a belief in the importance of culture for creating thriving cities while Eurocities is bringing together the local governments of over 130 of Europe's largest cities and 40 partner cities which,

between them, have 130 million citizens.[98] One of the most recent networks is The Global Parliament of Mayors[99] inspired by the ideas of Benjamin Barber, author of the book 'If Mayors Ruled the World' This is based on the view that cities, and the mayors that run them, offer the best new forces of good governance and best practices to support and accelerate global answers in an ever interdependent world. Greater and deeper collaboration is clearly the new normal.

**Co-opetition**

So how does ever-greater competition and deeper collaboration between cities actually work? What is the right balance? In the world of business, co-opetition – simultaneous competition and cooperation – is an important strategy that goes beyond the conventional rules of competition and cooperation to achieve advantages of both. Sharing supply chains, common platforms and defining new standards within an industry are all growing examples of this. For cities, parallel approaches are now emerging. In the UK, Liverpool and Manchester, established long-term competitors, are collaborating on a number of initiatives including one of several 'Cities for Business' partnerships where they are working together in the best interests of the North West region.[100] In Germany, cities in the Ruhr region are collectively promoting its sports and other cultural centres. Elsewhere in Europe cities such as Barcelona and Vienna are joining together to woo attractive global conferences for long-term collaborations. In Asia, competing Chinese cities are increasing co-branding in order to create momentum and attract investment. In addition, several regional tourism destinations are experimenting with new strategies where cooperation and co-opetition co-exist.

If we are going to tackle some of the challenges identified in our discussions, it is clear that **more widespread co-opetition is going to be a key part of the solution.** Addressing inequality, migration and scaling requires greater sharing of the best approaches. Equally, if we are to realize the ambitions of healthier, accessible and more intelligent cities, new ideas that link together the needs of not one, but multiple urban environments should be shared.

# Moving Forward

**The insights gained to date on the future of cities have helped us to clarify the main issues, highlight numerous examples and lay out a view of the landscape. As we take this project further with more discussions in Europe and Asia planned throughout 2017/18, we wish to focus on new solutions, identifying opportunities for innovation in planning, policy, strategy and collaboration. Collectively we seem to be clear on the problems, the causes and some of the off-the shelf answers. However, given the scale of both the challenges and the ambitions, new thinking is also going to be part of the mix.**

While we all recognise that every city is singular and so they have different set of problems and specific solutions, there are a number of common issues, concerns, ambitions and emerging challenges. Some of these are already being explored in depth by new collaborations – resilient cities, healthy cities and safe cities are all top of mind here. Other issues are being led by or promoted by a multitude of parties – intelligent cities and more innovative cities are, for example, both high on many agendas. Several new partnerships are now emerging to explore these further and we hope to help seed and guide some of these discussions using the insights gained to date. In addition, there are cross cutting topics like social cohesion, tolerance and openness to migration. These are increasingly political matters in many societies but with growing urbanisation a clear global trend for now and the future, they will have to be better addressed if more of us are going to live in close proximity to others.

While we recognise that there are many excellent research projects underway exploring elements of the future of cities, both globally and regionally, we hope that the insights the Future Agenda programme has gleaned and shared help.

# Research Methodology

**The Future of Cities is influenced by myriad issues beyond urban planning, the design of buildings and the creation of public spaces. From discussions around the future of water, food and energy to the future of transport, migration and health, the future how, why and where we live, as well as the 'who' is changing rapidly across multiple dimensions. As such, to gain a broad, global informed view on the key drivers of change the topic was embedded in the world's largest open foresight programme – Future Agenda.**

The Future Agenda programme is based on the idea that by engaging with others from different cultures, disciplines and industries, we can collectively create a more informed understanding of the world in which we live. This makes it easier to shape a strategy that will help to address the major challenges we face. Our aim is to identify ways in which systems could function, consumers behave and governments regulate over the next decade, and give all organisations, large or small, access to insights that we hope, will help them to develop their future strategy.

In the first Future Agenda programme, in 2010, an initial perspective on the future of cities was used to initiate discussions. This was authored by Ricky Burdett, Professor of Urban Studies at the London School of Economics and Political Science (LSE) and director of LSE Cities[101] and Urban Age[102] research projects. It was then taken around the world and built upon in discussions in key locations including Mumbai and London. Subsequent insights were shared in the World in 2020 book and website.[103] Adding onto this, we then also ran events in New York and Vienna to bring in additional views of urban development.

For the second Future Agenda programme in 2015 Harry Rich, CEO of the Royal Institution of British Architects (RIBA), authored another initial perspective.[104] This too was used as stimulus for multiple discussions and workshops that were conducted in Christchurch, Delhi, Singapore, London and Dubai and then, for additional views during 2016, in Singapore as well as in Beirut, Lebanon and Guayaquil, Ecuador. In 2017, we again ran an event in London and also added in other discussions in Toronto, Kuala Lumpur and Vienna. These assorted locations were chosen to ensure a range of views from cities of different sizes, in varied states of transition and facing diverse issues. Whilst not covering every possible urban typology to the extent of some studies, we feel that the discussions from this combination of cities have given us insights from a notably broad church. Adding into the mix other city-related views gained from the 100 or so other workshops undertaken on the future of water, food, resources, transport, trade, energy, migration, health, ageing, education and wealth, then, in total, we have identified around 150 different issues of relevance. These have been shared online in varied formats on different platforms and have since also gained further feedback. Lastly, we also included city-related questions in a major consumer survey undertaken in partnership with YouGov interviewing thousands of individuals in ten countries (USA, UK, Indonesia, China, India, Saudi Arabia, Russia, Australia, Brazil and Morocco). Together the views gained from thousands of different experts in 45 locations around the world provide the insights on the future of cities from which we have drawn this summary.

# References

1. www.futureagenda.org
2. http://www.geohive.com/cities/agg2016_2030.aspx
3. http://www.economist.com/news/leaders/21647614-poor-land-use-worlds-greatest-cities-carries-huge-cost-space-and-city
4. www.futureagenda.org
5. https://lsecities.net
6. http://www.un.org/en/development/desa/population/publications/policy/world-population-policies-2013.shtml
7. http://mirror.unhabitat.org/pmss/listItemDetails.aspx?publicationID=3386&AspxAutoDetectCookieSupport=1
8. IOM / Gallup (2015). How the World Views Migration. See www.publications.iom.int/system/files/how_the_world_gallup.pdf
9. http://www.solidere.com/city-center/urban-overview/master-plan
10. https://www.oecd.org/migration/OECD%20Migration%20Policy%20Debates%20Numero%202.pdf
11. http://urban-links.org/looking-beyond-quito%E2%80%8A-%E2%80%8Athe-u-s-agency-international-development-new-urban-agenda/
12. http://www.nber.org/papers/w13982
13. http://www.cbpp.org/research/poverty-and-inequality/a-guide-to-statistics-on-historical-trends-in-income-inequality
14. http://blog.euromonitor.com/2013/03/the-worlds-largest-cities-are-the-most-unequal.html
15. http://eprints.lse.ac.uk/69905/1/Burdett_Infrastructures%20of%20equality%20versus%20inequality_published_2017%20LSERO.pdf
16. https://www.theguardian.com/business/2015/jan/19/global-wealth-oxfam-inequality-davos-economic-summit-switzerland
17. https://www.oxfam.org/en/research/wealth-having-it-all-and-wanting-more
18. https://en.wikipedia.org/wiki/White_flight
19. http://dolphinliving.com/wp-content/uploads/FINAL-Estimating-the-Value-of-Discounted-Rental-Accommodation-2016.pdf
20. file:///Users/carolinejones/Downloads/Urban-World-Global-Consumers-Executive-summary.pdf
21. https://www.brookings.edu/research/city-and-metropolitan-inequality-on-the-rise-driven-by-declining-incomes/
22. http://blog.euromonitor.com/2013/03/the-worlds-largest-cities-are-the-most-unequal.html
23. http://citiespapers.ssrc.org/notes-on-neighborhood-inequality-and-urban-design/
24. https://www.lincolninst.edu/subcenters/atlas-urban-expansion/google-earth-data.aspx
25. https://www.weforum.org/agenda/2016/05/africa-biggest-cities-fragility/
26. http://www.citylab.com/work/2012/03/are-satellite-cities-cities-future/1468/
27. https://www.amsterdam.nl/wonen-leefomgeving/structuurvisie/structural-vision-am/
28. https://www.ura.gov.sg/uol/master-plan.aspx?p1=View-Master-Plan
29. https://www.london.gov.uk/what-we-do/planning/london-plan
30. http://www.futureagenda.org/insight/air-quality
31. http://www.wsj.com/articles/singapores-air-quality-plummets-as-haze-returns-1472187305
32. http://berkeleyearth.org/air-pollution-and-cigarette-equivalence/
33. http://www.bbc.co.uk/news/world-europe-38078488
34. http://www.economist.com/blogs/economist-explains/2016/10/economist-explains-2
35. http://www.bbc.co.uk/news/science-environment-38170794
36. http://www.ucsusa.org/clean-vehicles/california-and-western-states/what-is-zev#.WDXYl3ecZdA
37. http://www.futureagenda.org/insight/eco-civilisation
38. http://www.gdrc.org/uem/water/watershed/urban-water-pollution.html
39. https://www.theguardian.com/weather/2014/sep/05/brazil-drought-crisis-rationing.
40. http://www.livescience.com/40983-worlds-10-worst-polluted-places.html

41 https://www.pub.gov.sg/watersupply/fournationaltaps/newater
42 https://soapboxie.com/social-issues/25-Most-Dirtiest-Cities-In-The-World
43 https://www.theguardian.com/lifeandstyle/2017/feb/14/sea-to-plate-plastic-got-into-fish
44 http://www.futureagenda.org/insight/urban-obesity
45 http://news.bbc.co.uk/1/hi/health/7151813.stm
46 https://en.wikipedia.org/wiki/Gezi_Park_protests
47 http://www.dezeen.com/2012/10/24/great-city-by-adrian-smith-gordon-gill-architecture/
48 https://www.theguardian.com/cities/2015/apr/28/end-of-the-car-age-how-cities-outgrew-the-automobile
49 http://www.economist.com/news/international/21595031-rich-countries-have-cut-deaths-and-injuries-caused-crashes-toll-growing
50 http://publications.arup.com/publications/c/cities_alive_towards_a_walking_world
51 http://inhabitat.com/how-the-cheonggyecheon-river-urban-design-restored-the-green-heart-of-seoul/
52 http://publications.arup.com/publications/s/shaping_ageing_cities
53 https://www.theguardian.com/cities/2016/apr/25/improving-with-age-how-city-design-is-adapting-to-older-populations
54 http://yalebooks.com/book/9780300204803/city-tomorrow
55 http://edition.cnn.com/2016/10/10/asia/yinchuan-smart-city-future/
56 http://anthonymobile.com
57 http://books.wwnorton.com/books/smart-cities/
58 https://www.theguardian.com/cities/2014/dec/17/truth-smart-city-destroy-democracy-urban-thinkers-buzzphrase
59 https://www.theguardian.com/cities/2014/jun/25/predicting-crime-lapd-los-angeles-police-data-analysis-algorithm-minority-report
60 https://vartree.blogspot.co.uk/2014/04/i-know-where-you-were-last-summer.html
61 https://www.bloomberg.com/news/articles/2013-06-04/putting-human-bodies-into-the-internet-of-things
62 http://senseable.mit.edu
63 http://unlistedvideos.com/v/youtube-wabynfxZNMw.html
64 http://yalebooks.com/book/9780300204803/city-tomorrow
65 http://safecities.economist.com/report/safe-cities-index-white-paper/
67 https://www.architecture.com/Files/RIBAHoldings/PolicyAndInternationalRelations/Policy/CounterTerrorism/RIBADesigningforCounterTerrorism.pdf
68 https://qz.com/733374/counter-terrorism-architecture-how-cities-prevent-attacks-without-looking-like-theyre-trying/
69 http://www.harvarddesignmagazine.org/issues/42/fortress-london-the-new-us-embassy-and-the-rise-of-counter-terror-urbanism
70 https://www.theguardian.com/uk-news/2016/dec/20/what-can-be-done-to-prevent-berlin-style-attacks-in-modern-cities
71 https://www.newscientist.com/article/dn27997-cyber-attack-how-easy-is-it-to-take-out-a-smart-city/
72 http://www.wsj.com/articles/cyberattacks-raise-alarms-for-u-s-power-grid-1483120708?mg=id-wsj
73 https://www.campbellcollaboration.org/news-archive/news/cctv-has-modest-impact-on-crime
74 http://www.100resilientcities.org/blog/entry/ten-cities-that-are-leading-on-climate-change#/-_/
75 https://www.siemens.com/press/pool/de/events/2014/infrastructure-cities/2014-06-CCLA/rio-climate-close-up.pdf
76 http://www.rioonwatch.org/?p=17687
77 https://www.jrf.org.uk/report/social-cohesion-diverse-communities
78 http://www.lse.ac.uk/resources/calendar/courseGuides/SO/2016_SO4A2.htm
79 http://www.futureagenda.org/insight/flooded-cities
80 https://www.weforum.org/agenda/2015/11/major-cities-under-water

81 http://www.nyc.gov/html/sirr/html/report/report.shtml
82 http://uccrn.org/arc3-2/
83 http://www.100resilientcities.org
84 https://www.rockefellerfoundation.org/report/city-resilience-framework/
85 http://www.100resilientcities.org/blog/entry/ten-cities-that-are-leading-on-climate-change#/-_/
86 https://www.munichre.com/us/weather-resilience-and-protection/about-wrap/index.html
87 http://www.100resilientcities.org/blog/entry/what-is-a-chief-resilience-officer1#/-_/
88 http://www.swissre.com/global_partnerships/Swiss_Re_and_partners_to_develop_resilience_bonds.html
89 http://documents.worldbank.org/curated/en/902411467990995484/Competitive-cities-for-jobs-and-growth-what-who-and-how
90 https://www.pwc.com/gx/en/government-public-sector-research/pdf/cities-final.pdf
91 http://ceoworld.biz/2016/12/02/indias-top-12-tech-cities-digital-indian-cities-survey-2016/
92 http://www.fdiintelligence.com/Rankings/fDi-s-Global-Cities-of-the-Future-2016-17-the-winners?ct=true
93 http://www.citylab.com/politics/2015/12/secrets-of-the-worlds-most-competitive-cities/420720/
94 http://www3.weforum.org/docs/GAC/2014/WEF_GAC_CompetitivenessOfCities_Report_2014.pdf
95 http://www.c40.org/networks
96 http://www.co-society.com/collaborative-cities-raise-less-collaborative-nations-stall/
97 http://www.theatlantic.com/business/archive/2015/05/when-cities-and-suburbs-work-together/391979/
98 https://www.thersa.org/discover/publications-and-articles/rsa-blogs/2015/04/the-rise-of-the-collaborative-city
99 https://globalparliamentofmayors.org
100 https://www.corecities.com/news-events/new-cities-business-partnership-launched-create-jobs-and-investment-outside-south-east
101 https://lsecities.net
102 https://urbanage.lsecities.net
103 http://archive.futureagenda.org/pg/cx/view/#0
104 https://www.architecture.com

# Tables and graph references

Source (i) **THE URBAN AND RURAL POPULATION OF THE WORLD, 1950-2030**

Source (ii) **CITIES WITH HIGHEST GINI COEFFIENTS**
http://blog.euromonitor.com/2013/03/the-worlds-largest-cities-are-the-most-unequal.html

Source (iii) **FASTING GROWING CITIES. Estimated Urban Growth 2016 to 2025**
https://www.weforum.org/agenda/2017/02/the-world-s-fastest-growing-cities/

Source (iv) **MAP OF SE CHINA CITIES NETWORK**
http://www.telegraph.co.uk/news/worldnews/asia/china/8278315/China-to-create-largest-mega-city-in-the-world-with-42-million-people.html

Source (v) **20 WORST CITIES FOR AIR POLLUTION**
http://www.who.int/phe/health_topics/outdoorair/databases/cities/en/

Source (vi) **CITY POPULATIONS IN WALKING DISTANCE OF RAIL AND METRO STATIONS**
https://lsecities.net/media/objects/articles/public-transport-accessibility-in-world-cities/en-gb/

Source (vii) **SMART CITY IDEAL**
https://connectedtechnbiz.files.wordpress.com/2014/10/smart-city-concept.jpg

Source (viii) **SAFEST CITIES FROM EIU INDEX**
http://safecities.economist.com/report/safe-cities-index-white-paper/

Source (ix) **WORLDS MOST AT-RISK CITIES FROM FLOODING**
http://www.livescience.com/38956-most-vulnerable-cities-to-flooding.html

Source (x) **THE CITY RESILIENCE FRAMEWORK**
https://www.rockefellerfoundation.org/report/city-resilience-framework/

www.ingramcontent.com/pod-product-compliance
Lightning Source LLC
Chambersburg PA
CBHW042025200526
45172CB00028B/1121